I SHALL WEAR PURPLE

By
Linda Mather

I shall wear purple

ISBN-13: 978-1479256259

Cover art by Dreamstime

I shall wear purple

Me wearing purple and being 'me'

Linda was born in Easington Colliery, Co Durham in 1958, she then moved to Leicester in the early 1960's, which is where she spent her childhood. But, it was in 'Shakespeare County,' Warwickshire, where she says she 'grew up' during and after completing her counselling diploma.

She is now an experienced counsellor, supervisor, & trainer, and a behavioural family therapist. She has three grown up children and eight grandchildren.

This is Linda's first of hopefully many self-help books. She is very passionate about developing both her own emotional growth, and assisting others in theirs.

This book is a dedication to all those who have allowed her to 'wear purple'

I shall wear purple

<u>To my parents Owen and Vera Williams</u>

"You have put love, grace and enthusiasm into the lives of your children, I am so glad you were my parents" and thank you Dad for being <u>my</u> Dad!

<u>To my children, Paul, Claire and Emma</u>
"The biggest lesson we have to give our children is truth; you all enriched my life and brought me great happiness"
Thank you for all the joys you have given me. Please be yourselves in a world that will try to change you. <u>I love you always and forever.</u>

<u>To my grandchildren, Chelsea, Charlotte, Scarlett, Emily, Isobel, Lacey, Farren, Poppy and Kaven and any more that may follow</u>
"Always be proud of who you are, because you are and always will be a gift to us all"

<u>To my friends who have contributed to this book, & my life and allowed me to 'wear purple' (You know who you are)</u> *"Some people come into our lives and leave footprints in our souls, and we are never, ever the same"*

PROLOGUE

WARNING

When I am an old woman I shall wear purple
With a red hat which does not go, and doesn't't suit me,
And I shall spend my pension on brandy and summer gloves
And satin sandals, and say we havee no money for butter.

I shall sit down on the pavement when I'm tired
And gobble up samples in shops and press alarm bells
And run my stick along the public railings
And make up for the sobriety of my youth.

I shall go out in my slippers in the rain
And pick the flowers in other peoples gardens
And learn to spit.
You can wear terrible shirts and grow more fat
And eat three pounds of sausages at a go
Or only bread and pickle for a week
And hoard pens and pencils and beer mats and things in boxes.

But now we must have clothes that keep us dry
And pay our rent and not swear in the street
And set a good example for the children.
We must have friends to dinner and read the papers.
But maybe I ought to practice a little now?
So people who know me are not too shocked and surprised
When suddenly I am old, and start to wear purple.

Jenny Joseph 1932

Prologue

I want to buy that bubble gum that I had as a kid, you remember the large pink stuff that cost about a penny. You could blow the most amazing bubbles, which almost covered your face. I want to stand in the middle of Asda and blow the largest bubble ever!

What stops me? I am a 53 year-old mother of three, a grandmother of eight. I am a counselor, a daughter, a sister, and a friend. It is not what I am supposed to do. It is not how others would expect me to behave. So do I live my life as I believe others want me to or do I stand in Asda and blow bubbles?

That is what this book is about, it is a journey through our lives to look at what has changed us from being who we really want to be, who we really are.

It help's us to understand the beliefs that we adapt, the feelings that we hide and the thoughts that effect the way that we feel. It helps us to take a look at how we behave due to these feelings and thoughts. It helps us to express the feelings that we feel unable to express It will demonstrate how we become the people that we think other people want us to be losing a sense of who we really are in the process.

Many self help books will promise you success, wealth, love or many wonderful things, if you just read the book. I find this difficult to understand, as human psychopathology is a very complex subject. Emotional intelligence and emotional growth is a life long journey, so I can't promise you this.

What I can promise you though is a 'tool' to help you on that journey, a different 'road' to travel by and a deeper understanding of your own pathology and ways in which to change the personality traits that you have developed over the years that are not helpful to you.

Somewhere along our life journey we lose our 'real selves' and become exhausted by the different masks that we wear. This can eventually lead to psychological illnesses such as depression, stress and anxiety. It can lead to substance misuse, broken relationships, anger, resentments and unfulfilling lives.

This book will help you to begin to drop some of those masks and be your own unique self. It will help you to begin to accept yourself and subsequently be accepted for who you are by significant others. It will enable you to begin to love freely, to offer acceptance to other people and in the process it will increase your energy levels, leaving you feeling more alive than you have in years.

Maybe when you have this energy you can then follow your dream of money, love, the ideal career etc. However, psychological pain depletes you of physical energy so work on ourselves is need first.

My motivation for writing this book is that we are living in an age where therapy is becoming more and more difficult to access, waiting lists are far too long and 'brief' therapy appears to be the answer to everyone's problems, I learned during my own therapeutic journey both as a client and as a therapist many tools that can help us to begin to learn more about ourselves and change the 'things' that are impacting on our lives in a negative way.

I wanted to share those tools with therapists and clients to empower people to get back in touch with their 'true selves.'

There is nothing wrong with being 'you'.

If you are feeling stuck and disillusioned with life. If you regularly feel that you can't relax and be yourself, are you feeling weary and don't know why, there's a good chance that you are habitually wearing different masks, you may not notice that you are doing it, you may have done it for most of your life.

You may be juggling these masks to hide your pain and in the process lose a sense of your own identity. This book helps you to identify those masks and begin a process of stripping down the defenses and find the 'you' that you love to be, the you that you were born to be, the you before all those painful things happened to you, the you that is hidden behind masks. Think of this as a journey of self discovery.

Although this book is by no means a tool to replace therapy as nothing can beat the process of a good therapeutic relationship and the excellent work that therapist's worldwide do. It is a tool to start you on that journey, to give you an insight into different therapeutic models and to give you an appreciation on what therapy is about, how it works and how it can change your life and the way that you function as a human being.

I would suggest that when reading this book you read one chapter at a time and digest this chapter before moving on to the next. Process the information; learn what the problem is before trying to fix it, after all if the washing machine breaks down you don't try and fix it before you troubleshoot do you. The same goes with our lives, spending some time troubleshooting will help you to fix the problem properly.

These symbols throughout the book are times when

you may want to stop and think. Process and trouble shoot & use the exercises on you. They will give you personal insight. Enjoy your journey!

What is also exciting about this book is that a lot of the tools can be used on clients, for those therapists or psychologists who are reading the book to help them to gain insight too.

Please spread the word of this book, let's see how many people we can reach, and I need you to keep me in supply of bubble gum please.

If I do decide to stand in Asda and blow the largest bubble ever, what will happen to me?

Will I die? Will I be sectioned to the nearest psychiatric hospital? Will I stop being loved or accepted?

Chances are I may get a few odd looks. Someone might laugh. I may even get envied for my sense of freedom, my ability to have fun. But nothing bad will happen to me.

So, if you see me in Asda blowing bubbles I hope that you will join me! And if you ever meet me, please give me permission to be 'me' as I will you.

DON'T BE FOOLED BY ME!

Don't be fooled by me. Don't be fooled by the mask I wear, for I wear a thousand masks, masks that I am afraid to take off, and none of them are me!
I give the impression that I'm secure, sunny and unruffled, within as well as without, that confidence is my name and coolness is my game, that the waters calm and I am in command, and that I need no-one. But don't believe me! My surface may seem smooth, but my surface is my mask.

Beneath dwells the real me in confusion, in fear and aloneness. But I hide this. I don't want anyone to know it. I panic at the thought of my weakness and fear of being exposed. That's why I frantically create a mask to hide behind, a sophisticated facade to help me to pretend, to shield me from the glance that knows. But such a glance is precisely my salvation, which is if it is followed by acceptance, if it is followed by love.

I'm afraid that you will think less of me that you will laugh at me and your laugh would kill me! I'm afraid that deep down I am nothing, that I'm no good, and that you will see this and reject me.
*So I play my desperate game, with a facade of assurance without and a trembling child within. **And so begins the parade of masks.** And my life becomes a front. I chatter idly to you of superficialities. I tell you everything that is really nothing, and nothing of what is everything-of what is crying within me.*

So when I am going through my routine, do not be fooled by what I am saying, what I'd like to be able to say, what, for survival, I need to say but can't. I dislike hiding-honestly! I dislike the phony game I am playing. I'd really like to be genuine and spontaneous - and me. You've got to hold out your hand, even when that is the last thing that I seem to want. Only you can call me to aliveness. Each time you are kind and gentle and encouraging, each time you try to understand because you really care, my heart begins to grow wings - very small wings, very feeble wings, but wings! With your sensitivity and sympathy and your power of understanding you can breathe life into me.

I want you to know that, I want you to know how important you are to me, how you can be the creator of the person that is me if you choose to. Please choose to. You alone can break down the wall behind which I tremble. You alone can remove my mask.

Please do not pass me by. It will not be easy for you. A long conviction of worthlessness builds strong walls, The more closely you approach me, the more blindly I strike back. But I am told that love is stronger than walls, and in this lies my hope. Please try to beat down those walls with firm hands - but with gentle hands.........for a child is very sensitive.

Who am I, you may wonder?
I am someone you know very well!
For I am every man that you meet,
and I am every woman that you meet!
Charles C Finn

Chapter One
"The masks we wear"

"We are all born free," says Eric Berne, the founder of Transactional Analysis. The world is a safe place as long as we have our basic needs met is the school of thought of many psychological theories. Therefore, we are not born with inbuilt prejudices or values. We are not born with an internal belief system.

We do not come out of our mother's womb thinking. *"It's not safe to get too close to the opposite sex, they let you down"* or *"It's not okay to show feelings such as anger or pain"*. We do not stand in front of a mirror at three months old and say *"Does my bum look big in this?"* So where do these values and beliefs come from?

They are values and beliefs that we develop or inherit as we grow; they come from messages we hear or think that we hear, and from our own personal experiences. They come from how we digest other people's reactions to us, how we internalize our world.

What would happen I wonder, if we remained *"free?"* How would we be? Who would we be? Would we be happier? Would our lives me more content? Would our relationships be healthier? Would the world that we live in be a better place?

That's something that we may never know, because it would be impossible for any of us not to develop some sort of internal belief system. However, it would be nice if we could get rid of some of the beliefs that hold us back. The ones that stop us from forming healthy relationships, and prohibit us from doing what

13

we really want to do. It would be so nice to see freer people in this world, people who are authentic and carefree.

Most of us can remember the little clichés that were used when we were children to encourage us to do the things we did not want to do, or to stop us from doing the things we did want to do.

"Eat all your vegetables," says Mother, *"or you will end up blind. You never see rabbits in the optician's do you?"*

No, we don't see rabbits in the opticians but as we grow older we eliminate that 'belief' by doing a 'reality check' - where's the evidence? Even if a rabbit was blind or losing his sight, he's hardly likely to put on his best suit and walk through the door of an optician.

These are what Eric Berne called 'contamination's' – they are messages that we have heard that had an effect on what we did, despite not wanting to do. Or what we did not do albeit wanting to. Of course, evidence tells us that vegetables are good for us. But what about the 'contamination's we receive that stop us from functioning healthily. Stop us from expressing emotions that are healthy to express.

Imagine you are two years old and you are angry because mum has put milk in your bottle and you wanted orange juice. We don't have the resources at two to say. *"Hey Mom, I'm angry with you right now, as you have given me milk instead of orange. Can you change it please"* so you throw the bottle across the room, the lid comes off and milk explodes all over mum's new carpet. Whoops! Gee moms mad and she gives you a huge smack on the backside.

It hurts like nothings ever hurt before, instead of the usual love in her eyes; you may see hatred and her anger. This is as painful as the smack on the backside, all we want as children, as human beings is love and acceptance. As children we all want mummy to be pleased with us, and learn from a very young age what it is we have to do to make Mum and Dad happy.

This experience, the experience of being smacked and unloved, may teach you that it's not okay around here to express anger, and you may begin to suppress your anger, after all you don't want to feel that pain again. Alas, the first mask appears **"The cool cucumber."**

> **Memory............. is the**
> **diary that we all carry about with us.**
> **Oscar Wilde**

Imagine falling over and hurting yourself and you cry. Mummy or Daddy say's to you *"Big boys/girls don't cry"* or Granny sits in her chair laughing at you, you may learn that it's not okay to cry around here. Or mummy says "Jump up shout sugar" or "Be a brave little soldier."

Another mask appears **"The tough cookie"** and so begins the parade of masks until you don't know who you are anymore. Until the masks disguise the real you.

Take a few minutes to think about the messages you received as a child. Then try to think about what mask or masks may have developed due this message.

When the **'tough cookie'** is worn, what might you do then with your 'anger' or 'sadness?'

Sometimes we may suppress this unacceptable feeling. Other times, we replace it with a feeling that is more acceptable within our personal 'world', like "Fear" or "Guilt" so instead of showing 'anger' we show 'guilt.' For some people 'fear' or 'guilt' is not acceptable in their 'world,' so they replace those feelings with other feelings such as 'anger' or 'sadness.'

Does this make you think about people's authenticity? Hiding behind acceptable feelings and hiding behind masks. How are people going to support us, understand us when we express a non-authentic 'feeling.' Is it surprising then that we often feel misunderstood? How wonderful it would be to be 'heard' or to be understood.

We often blame other's for this, *"My wife does not understand me"* or *"Why does no-one ever listen to me?"* and yet it is our responsibility if we are misunderstood because if we are not saying what we are really feeling, and if we are not 'being' who we really are how can we be totally understood.

Here is a story that you may be familiar with; a man comes home from work; he has just heard that a colleague had seen his wife having lunch with another man, three days ago.

He walks in the door and shouts and yells because the kid's toys are all over the living room floor. His wife is shocked. This has never bothered him before; in fact he'd always said that kids should be allowed to play freely in the home. She cannot understand why it has suddenly become an issue. Later that evening, he snapped at her for turning the television on to another channel, even though he was not watching it. Again, his wife is confused. They go to bed in silence. The following day is much of the same, causing more puzzlement for his poor wife.

Three days later, he says what he is really angry about, (his wife being out with another man), his wife explains that she had bumped into her brother in town and had a quick lunch with him.

This man demonstrated unauthentic feelings, he projected his feelings of anger onto the children and their toys and his wife and her channel hopping. Is it possible that 'jealousy' was the forbidden feeling in this guy's world? If only he had been able to express this in the beginning, if only he had been able to be more authentic, then their marriage would not have been in turmoil for three days! Three days that will be part of this couples history, part of what might create more 'masks.'

It's strong people who have the courage to show their vulnerability

We are all unique and have experienced unique histories, therefore we will all be different in what feelings that we will express or show to other people, particularly people we care about and people that we are trying to impress.

In our world growing up, we may have learned which feelings are acceptable in our family and which are not. The ones that are not are then kept hidden by a mask.

Let's suppose that most negative feelings such as anger, hurt, jealousy and helpless are feelings we were told not to feel for some reason or another, or received a negative experience when expressing those feelings. This is when we start wearing masks to then hide those feelings. This is when we start expressing inauthentic feelings, that do not express how we really feel.

In this book I will demonstrate to you how those unauthentic feelings that we reveal to others to cover up our real feelings create us many more problems than our authentic feelings ever would.

Have a think about what are your 'forbidden feelings?'

- Are they feelings that you expressed in the past that triggered a negative response?
- What bad thing might happen if you express these feelings?
- Will something good happen if you have the courage to 'be real about how you are feeling?

To help you here is a feeling list. Try ringing the ones that you rarely or do not show:

Mad, Sad, Scared, Joyful, Powerful, Peaceful, Thoughtful, Content, Sleepy, Bored, Lonely, Depressed, Ashamed, Guilty, Hurt, Hostile, Angry, Rage, Hateful, Critical, Rejected, Confused, Helpless, Submissive. Insecure, Anxious, Excited, Sexy, Energetic, Playful, Creative, Aware, Proud, Respected, Appreciated, Hopeful, Important, Faithful, Nurturing, Trusting, Loving, Intimate, Bashful, Stupid, Miserable, Inadequate, Inferior, Apathetic, Pensive, Relaxed, Responsive, Serene, Sentimental, Thankful, Confident, Intelligent, Worthwhile, Valuable, Satisfied, Cheerful, Delightful, Extravagant, Amused, Stimulating, Fascinating, Daring, Embarrassed, Foolish, Weak, Insignificant, Discouraged, Bewildered, Skeptical, Irritated, Furious, Frustrated, Selfish, Jealous.

Look at the 'feelings' that you very rarely show and ask yourself why?

- Are they forbidden feelings?
- Feelings that you believe are unsafe to show?
- Are they feelings that were discouraged in your family?
- Are they feelings that you once showed but instigated a negative response from others?

These masks that hide our true feelings are there for a purpose, we believe they protect us from getting hurt, but do they? Or do they set us up for further pain? I will show you in this book how the later is usually the case. I will demonstrate to you how the masks we develop can in most cases do us more harm than good. How they assist us in attracting the wrong people. How they enable us to avoid intimacy and how they cause us psychological distress. **The masks we use to protect us can actually stop us from living a healthy life to the full.**

Ask yourself these questions

- Are there times when you can't be honest about how you feel?
- When you are in company do you sometimes feel strained and uncomfortable and unable to relax?
- Has anyone ever described you one way and then when they got to know you a bit better, realized that you were

another way?

- Do you act as though you don't care what others say or thing about you, but deep down it hurts like hell?
- Has anyone ever commented or are you aware that you act differently with different people?

Chances are you are wearing masks, several masks in fact. Most people want to see you, and yet you are hiding behind a false persona to protect yourself from pain, but the truth is the masks you wear are causing you more pain.

I would like you to think about our uniqueness, think about how different we all are. Do you ever notice how two, three or more children from the same parentage can all be so different in personality? How these same children will have a different view of their childhood? They will have a different view of their world? This is because we all internalise our experiences differently, we perceive covert and overt messages from our caretakers differently and our individual personalities develop from those experiences.

That is also why our children often have very different personalities from each other. They have internalized some of both parent's qualities and developed some of their own due to how they have interpreted their world.

This is a true story:

Two children from the same family were encouraged to do things by their parents by comparing them with other children. Father would say,

"Come on Johnny let's take your stabilisers off your bike, little Jimmy across the road is younger than you and he can ride his bike without his stabilisers on."

Innocent words of encouragement by a caring father, and yet

both these children internalised these messages in a different way.

Johnny grew up to be a high achiever always wanting to be better than other people (other Jimmy's) and yet his brother spent most of his life on benefits because there were always little Jimmy's in the world that could do things a whole lot better.

Both these children had internalized their father's encouragement in a different way.

This is why we can never be 'perfect' parents; we can only do our best because our children will internalize what we say and what we do into their own frame of reference. We can only do our best as a parent and be 'real' ourselves. Which in itself will encourage our children to be 'real' too? We can also allow them to express 'real' feelings.

Each day of our lives we make deposits in the memory banks of our children. - Charles R Swindoll

Our experiences are what help us to decide what masks we wear and what beliefs we adapt, what feelings, thoughts or behaviours that we can or can't show and what feelings, thoughts or behaviours are not safe to share, hiding our true selves from the world. We learn what is accepted in our world and equally what is not, we then adapt to be what is expected of us.

When they have fixed a new speed camera at the top of your road and you are unaware of it, you drive past and it flashes, resulting in a £60 fine and points on your license. Do you do it again and again? Most people usually adapt their behaviours to drive more safely, (if only when they know where the speed cameras are).

So, imagine in Middle school you are asked to stand up and talk about a particular project you have done. At the end instead of the anticipated applause, the whole class laughs at you - what are the chances of you ever speaking in public again? You will adapt your behaviour to avoid re-experiencing this awful time.

This one experience could have stopped you from 'being' who you really are, who you really want to be. It may create for you anxiety in later life, when asked to speak in front of a few or many people. It may create a 'fear' of getting things 'wrong,' a fear of being laughed at, so it becomes safer for you to do nothing at all. This experience could have changed your whole life plan. What might you have done if you had not had this one 'bad' experience? Who might you have been?

These experiences are what help us to create our masks; the masks that we believe will protect us. We are often not consciously aware of some of the masks that we wear or that we have developed over the years.

These masks exhaust us, deplete us of physical energy.

Have you ever been part of a show, involved in amateur dramatics or played a role in a school play? Can you remember, or imagine how exhausted you felt after each performance, when for two or three hours you have been Oliver in Oliver twist or Annie or any other fictitious character.

Can you remember or imagine coming off the stage and feeling exhausted and relieved that the show was over and that you could be 'you' again?

Then how exhausted must you feel with the roles that you play in your own life because of your perceived expectations of what others want you to be. You must be worn out!

Stop and think for a moment about the times you have been on a boy or girl's night out or a business dinner with the boss, or even a hot date. You return home alone and you put your key in the door. Can you remember how you felt? Did you feel your shoulders drop? Did you feel an overwhelming sense of tiredness but at the same time relaxed? That's usually because the 'show' is over. When you walk into the house you can at last be 'you' again!

I spent half of my life trying to be who I thought other people wanted me to be, my friends my family, my colleagues until one day it just got too much. It did not stop me from being hurt or rejected. It did not make me any more liked. It actually created more pain and rejection and resulted in depression. After the third day of laying in bed feeling like my world had collapsed, I got up and said, *"Today I am going to wear purple - today I am going to be me!"* and I have never looked back.

Every morning this is my mantra and I have never felt so loved and respected as I do now. It's true that some people may not like or accept the new 'me' and may reject the 'real me' but it appears to be far less than those who rejected the 'phony' me.

When you are content to be simply yourself and don't compare or compete, everybody will respect you. - Lao Tzu

I have lost count of the number of clients I see who try so hard to be who they perceive other people want them be. I have seen clients who use cocaine to 'keep up' with the expectations they put on themselves, to keep going to impress others. I have treated clients who use cannabis, heroin, and alcohol because life has become too hard, too difficult to meet everyone's expectations of them.

We live in a world where it is important to 'fit in', to achieve, to be liked, to be accepted and we try so hard to do all of these things, that it all becomes too much.

I have experienced people who use drugs and alcohol excessively because it allows them to be themselves for a while, or blots out the negative feelings from trying to be who others expect them to be. After all, it's okay to make a fool of yourself when drunk or stoned or show your true feelings or express your thoughts because if there is any risk of hurt or rejection, well let's face it we can always blame it on the 'substance.'

More and more people are presenting with drug and alcohol problems, we treat them, and some may judge them. Agencies will often treat the 'addiction' but rarely explore the underlying reasons to their use. Often people with addictions are not aware of the reasons that they use, they just know it makes them feel better, it is however a quick fix.

This is why it is important in addiction treatment to explore with the client their belief system, their behaviors, feelings, their histories and their personalities. Not just their drug use.

Substance misuse can create feelings of anxiety, depression, stress and obsessive beliefs. The drug and alcohol use then increases to manage more painful feelings and the cycle goes on.

More and more people are presenting with mental health problems that services are struggling to cope. How many of them are burnt out from wearing masks? Or anxious at the thought of dropping those masks, for fear of rejection, abandonment or abuse?

How many hold on to unresolved feelings or pain from the past? How many are experiencing 'burn out' from juggling all those masks? How many are struggling in interpersonal relationships?

Is your life how another person or other people want it to be? How many people know the 'real' you?

It is amazing how much support you will get if you tell the truth! If you just be yourself.

Day in day out we are being who we think other people want us to be. We are on the stage of life playing out different roles. Is it any wonder we live in a society where stress mental illness and substance misuse is becoming more and more prevalent!

Is it society that is expecting perfectionism, or do we perceive that we have to be perfect to survive in today's society? More and more people are refusing to work, do we ever ask why? Could it be because wherever they work they have to 'be,' who others want them to be? If people could go to work and be 'themselves,' do you think they would enjoy it more? Would employers get more out of their workforce?

Imagine this day:

Diary

9.00a.m	*Meeting with manager*
12.00noon	*Lunch with colleagues*
2.00p.m	*Consultation with client*
4.00p.m.	*Tea with parents*
8.00p.m.	*Night out with .friends*

How many different roles will you play in this day? How many different masks will you wear?

- The eager hardworking employee.
- The supportive colleague.
- The professional
- The perfect child
- The belle of the ball/comedian.'

When is it okay to be just you?   When you walk through that door into an empty home?   How nice it would be to be able to be 'you' all day? Try it tomorrow and see what happens

Of course, we all have professional hats to wear, but 'hats' are very different to 'masks' - you can be yourself in a hat. 'Masks' are what we hide behind, they present something different to who we really are and can very often set us up for failure. They are phony and they are not the 'real you.'

We **can** be our real selves and still be accepted by others. Let's face it no-one likes a phony so why do we spend half our lives being one and hiding our true selves? Do you want to continue being a phony or are you ready to that the risk and be your true self?

How much are we doing for others? How much are we doing in our lives that we don't really want to do and how much time would we have for the things that we do want to do if we stopped doing what we don't want to do?

I worked with a client who really wanted to do something different with her life, but just could never seem to get started. We explored how she always stood at the bottom of a hill looking up at her goals but never started to climb the hill not even when setting herself mini-goals.

This was her hill:

> "I want to be a doctor or a teacher, I need to enrol on an access course, then I need to take driving lessons and get a car. I then need to do a degree at University. After this I will get married and have a family."

On exploration she discovered that actually this was not her goal, she just felt that she should do this because this was what all her friends had done, this was what her family wanted her to do, and this was in fact their goals for her!

We looked at **her** goals & **her** dreams for the future. Look at the difference!!

> "I would like to do some volunteer work, take my driving lessons, go to college to learn languages and then I would love to travel before I have a family.

Notice how in the second statement she uses "I would like….. I would love……. Compared to the first where she uses words such as "I want….. I need……." Is it any wonder that she could never get started on climbing that first hill if it was not really what she wanted? Of course she is going to climb half way up the hill and fall back down again when its not what she really wants.

Could she be unconsciously or perhaps consciously sabotaging herself?

Are you following the goals/dreams of what others or you perceive others to expect of you.

Give yourself permission to follow your own!

PERSONAL NOTES & EXCERCISES:

Chapter Two
"Relationships"

ONE PERFECT ROSE

A single flow'r he sent me, since we met,
All tenderly his messenger he chose;
Deep-hearted, pure, with scented dew still wet -
One perfect rose.

I knew the language of the floweret;
'My fragile leaves,' it said, 'his heart enclose.'
Love long has taken for his amulet
One perfect rose

Why is it no one ever sent me yet
One perfect limousine, do you suppose?
Ah no, it's always just my luck to get
One perfect rose.

Dorothy Parker - 1893-1967

If we present ourselves in one way, then how can we be disappointed in the results we get from that presentation?

Think about all the times that you have met new people. This could be potential partners, work colleagues, lovers or friends. How often do we show them our 'real selves?'

Why don't we? What do we fear happening if we do?

In the past when we have shown the parts of us that we now keep hidden, this has usually resulted in a negative experience. We may have been laughed at or rejected or disliked or even looked at with disdain. These actions by others can leave us with 'bad' feelings about ourselves and lower our self esteem. It is natural that we are going to do all that we can to prevent ourselves from feeling the same again. So we will desperately try to cover that 'side' of us up.

We may worry that by showing this 'hidden part' people might not like us, and if they don't like us they may reject us, and worse they may manipulate other people to not like us or reject us too. We may feel that people who see our true self might abuse us, they may abandon us or they may even engulf us.

These experiences have usually happened to us before, in the past, otherwise we would not know how painful or uncomfortable they are. We would not need to protect ourselves from pain, if we did not know what pain felt like. Therefore, to avoid this happening, we will present in a way that we feel will stop this from happening to us again.

We will present in a way that we think people want us to. But does it, does it stop the pain?

If you think about something that you find painful for example: rejection, being lied to, being left out, being given the silent treatment. Does it happen to you over and over again?

If the answer is 'Yes' then ask yourself do these masks you are wearing really help? Have they prevented you from these painful experiences? The answer is usually "no" they just make us more resentful "I have tried my best and this still happens to me?"

For example at 12 years of age you experienced something bad when you said "no" to something, you were rejected in a big way. This is likely to lead you into wearing a '**People pleasing**' mask, for the rest of your life for fear of further rejection.

Therapists often explore the past with you, as uncomfortable as this may be sometimes, it helps both you and the therapist to see how the past is affecting relationships in the present, and will continue to affect the future unless changes are made. I do not feel that it is always necessary to stay in the past but it does help to explore your history to develop an understanding of the impact that the past has on you now. This then helps you to make changes.

Now let's explore what masks that you might wear in relationships:

We all have a social mask that we put on. We go out wear our best image. However, behind that social mask is a personal truth, which is what we really believe about who we are and what we are capable of.

Who are you and what social mask do you wear when you are out on the dating scene?

I shall wear purple

Are you the belle of the ball, the break dancing king, the comedian, tart with a heart, classy miss or the wallflower that sits in the corner people watching?

If you have a history of attracting the 'wrong' people reading this chapter will help you to define and understand the type of person you are attracting and why.

For all those married or committed readers, don't scrap this chapter as it can help you to look at why you attract the 'wrong' friends, and why people treat you in the way they do. I will be able to demonstrate to you how it is simply down to the way you present yourself, out of awareness of course.

We often attract people with the mask that we wear and boy what a disappointment they will get when that mask falls off.

Later in this book I will explore with you how relationships from the past can affect the way you relate to some people in the present. But first let's look at the 'dating game':

Jo and Phil are getting ready for a night out.

Jo is a homely, peaceful girl, that likes nothing more than cosy nights in with her partner. She likes to read poetry and relax listening to music.

She loves nights in with a good film, a take-away and a bottle of wine.

She enjoys walks in the park hand in hand on a warm summers day, and nights out at the theatre.

Her ideal man is a 'strong independent type that will take care of her and help improve the home that they live in.

AND

> *Phil is a needy type that likes being looked after.*
> *He enjoys football, quiz nights, nights out with the lads and boozy nights out with his partner.*
> *He hates DIY.*
> *His ideal woman is a strong independent type that has a strong mind and likes nothing more than to 'take care of her man!*

Both of these people have past experiences of rejection. Due to this their biggest fear was being rejected.   So to prevent themselves from being rejected, they do not show their 'real selves'.   They   fear not being liked and subsequently being rejected. So.............

Jo puts on her 'strong independent party animal' mask

Phil put's on his 'strong, independent, romantic, calm and smooth' mask

They meet. Wow! It's love at first sight.

    "Here is someone who can take care of me, someone I can snuggle up on the sofa with at night" thinks Jo.

    "Here is someone I can have fun and boozy nights out with and someone who won't make many demands on me" thinks Phil.

The dates begin.........

    Things are fine at first because both are wearing their social masks.   Perhaps even being who they think the other person wants them to be. Eventually though as their relationship develops their 'true self', their real needs will come out.

This is when the arguments begin..............

Phil wants to go out all the time; he's bored with cozy nights in and thinks 'why should anyone want to walk in the park hand in hand when there is a football match on at the local pub?'

Jo cannot understand why Phil wants to be out every night on booze ups with his mates, when they can have a romantic night in with a DVD and take-away.

Both are frustrated because they felt lied to, and they were in a sense, neither presented the true picture of who they really are. Both of them were being phony.

Unfortunately, it was how they perceived each other to be due to the social masks each of them wore at their initial meeting and follow up dates. As they got to know each other the masks slipped and each did not like what they saw below these social masks. They had not met their ideal date; in fact they were not suited to each other at all. Underneath their masks they both had very different ideas of what they wanted from a relationship.

Oh what a tangled web we weave when first we practice to deceive! - Sir Walter Scott

What a mess wearing these masks have created for this couple, I wonder what masks they will wear now, due to the pain of this relationship breakdown? Both feeling rejected again and possibly blaming each other for not meeting each other's needs. By wearing their masks they both set themselves up for what they both most feared and that was 'rejection'.

With their social mask being completely out of awareness they may continue to attract the wrong people by the masks they continue to wear, setting themselves up for one rejection after another.

Think of all the 'strong independent types that like cozy nights in and walks in the park hand in hand' that pass Jo by because they think she's an 'independent party animal.'

Guys who like cozy nights in and to be able to 'do things' for a woman, see Jo as a woman that likes to be out partying and possibly think "what does this independent woman need from me, what can I give her".

Phil possibly does not attract his ideal mate either because he presents as a romantic 'night in' type of guy and girls that like to party would not be attracted to him.

CAKE
I wanted one life you wanted another. We could not have our cake so we ate each other! - Roger McGough 1937

Will Phil and Jo ever meet their soul mate? They will one day when they come to an awareness of the masks that they wear when they are trying to attract a potential partner. When they one day learn to present as their 'true selves'.

How can we find a partner or friend who we are truly compatible with when we wear these 'social masks?' How can we develop relationships that last? We need to be truly happy with whom we really are, what we really need and then we need to present as this to the world.

Think about your own 'past' relationships that have now ended. Were you the 'real you' at the beginning of the relationship? Did the relationship end when you showed the 'real' you?

When we go into new relationships we often take the 'baggage' from an old relationship with us, whether that is 'good' baggage or 'bad' baggage. We can make the false assumption that any new person we meet will be the same as people from our past. This will just persuade you to keep up a guard, a mask.

Sometimes in or out of awareness we may 'test' the new relationships.

For example often people who have experienced domestic violence in a relationship, will push their new partners to the limit to see if they hit them. If they do then this will reinforce their belief that all men are bad and not enable them to see that their own presentation is possibly attracting this type of character.

No woman or man deserves to be hit, but there are people out there that do use their fists in anger and we need to ensure that we do not present in a way in which we may attract them into our lives.

Sometimes we may play games in relationships to gain love, attention and reassurance, or to get what we want without saying what we want directly or to avoid facing the truth. Games just cause further pain. Direct honest communication is the healthiest way to relate. This is who I am, this is what I need and this is what I want in this relationship. How about you?

Never let too much of yesterday use up too much of today. Dump that baggage in the nearest refuse bin and enter a new relationship freely. Go into it being your' true self' and expressing your 'true wants.' If you are not loved for that, then it is because that person is looking for something different in a relationship.

Remember that once your heart has been broken it grows back bigger. So if you are on the dating scene, or even if you're not, next time you go into a social situation where you meet new people throw away those masks and be yourself. Try it, it will amaze you how many people you attract because they like you. The 'real' you!

A mature relationship will be based on meeting each other 'freely' without taking with it the luggage from the past. How can you smell like a rose, when you live in the garbage of the past? Mature relationships accept each other as they find each other and they encourage independence. Mature relationships are open and honest from the start. They are about 'love' and not 'need' and they occur when we have emotional and mental balance. People in mature relationships do not play games, they ask for love, attention and reassurance, they face the truth and say what their fears are and they ask directly for what they need.

To do this, however we need to be happy being who we are instead of role-modeling ourselves on who we think we should be for others.

Love is not a bandage to cover wounds
Source unknown

So, dump those masks? If someone falls in love with you or likes you, they like you for who you are presenting.

If they fall in love with your 'mask' then that's the person they like and when the masks slip which they will, you are not then the person they fell for. Therefore all sorts of attempts will be made to 'change you' back to the person they believed you were.

How often do we hear when relationships have gone sour "S/he tried to change me?"

If you are your 'true self' that they like/fall in love with, they will not need to change you. They will love you, as you are 'YOU!'

Try not to fall victim to your own negative thoughts and feelings about yourself. Try not to hide the 'parts of yourself' that you feel others will not accept. Those parts are not to be ashamed of they are part of what makes us 'real' and unique. Remember we are not all perfect. We all have a shadow side, times when we are imperfect that's okay, it's what makes us human. Be human.

If you ask most people what they want in a relationship, somewhere near the top of their list is 'honesty and openness,' yet most of us do not begin a relationship in this way. Pretending is not being open and honest. Being who you believe they want you to be is not being open and honest. Wearing a mask is not being open and honest.

When we were 'little' we learned that if we behaved in a certain way, we got rewards such as hugs and kisses. This does not always work when we are 'grown up'. Besides do we want to get hugs and kisses for how we believe 'others' want us to be, or do we want more genuine hugs and kisses for being ourselves?

Do we want 'phony' hugs and kisses?

'Being the 'phony' you will only attract 'phony' hugs and kisses. It is much nicer to be loved for the person you are, not the person you are pretending to be.

If you were short you could not make yourself taller, so why try to make yourself anything other than who you are.

Be you, because you are lovely!

I wonder if she'd like me if I stood a little taller.
I wonder if she'd like me if my ears were only smaller.
Or maybe if I brushed my hair and gave her a red rose,
or if I changed my underwear and didn't pick my nose.
Perhaps if I could ride a mule. Perhaps if I could dance.
Perhaps if I could come to school in polka dotted pants.
Perhaps if I would shine my shoes and even wear a tie,
or if I wrestled kangaroos or sang a lullabye.
Or maybe if I built a ship and sailed the seven seas with
nothing but a paper clip and tubs of cottage cheese.
I wonder if she'd like me for the reasons I have listed.
I wonder if she'd like me if she knew that I existed. - Eric Ode

I often get asked "surely if you are showing your true self, this leaves you open to abuse, laying yourself bare, showing your vulnerabilities?"

Dropping your mask is not about revealing to people your 'crumple buttons' - showing them the parts of yourself that hurt, disclosing what hurts you, particularly not at the early stages of a relationship. This is intimacy and something you may want to reveal once a relationship has developed.

Intimacy is not for every relationship. You do not have to lay your heart bare for everyone that you meet. That is not always healthy. Intimacy is different for every relationship.

What I am suggesting is about 'being you' - Often we will pick up what a person wants in another i.e. "This guy likes girls to be homely and feminine, or sporty and fun." Don't try to be that, if that's not who you are, because that's being phony. Be who you are!

How many people do you know that are happily married and say *"I did not like him/her when we first met"* That's probably because they did not like the 'mask.' but liked what was underneath. Think about the times that you have met someone and taken an instant dislike to him or her, and then they have 'grown on you'. That might be because you did not like their mask.

Another common question is "What if I show my true self, stop wearing a mask and the people I meet continue to wear theirs?"

Practicing removing your masks with others is all about learning to be transparent. To be transparent we need to practice being accepting of others, as you accept other people for who 'they are,' they are more likely to begin to drop their masks.

From my experience, if you are authentic then others start to be too. If you are accepting of yourself, it encourages others to be likewise.

Imagine being sat on the beach with someone you don't know too well. It is a hot day and you are both fully clothed and sweltering in the heat. One of you starts stripping down to your bathing costume, what's the betting the other one follows suit soon after.

It is the same when you go to a club or out dancing, once one or two people get up to dance, within no time at all the whole dance floor is full. It takes one person to make the first move. Try making the first move.

When couples meet they often spend the first few months going to pubs, discos, or the cinema. This is better than jumping into bed on the first date I guess, but it does not allow you to get to know each other, to get to know the real person. Getting to know each other takes communication. The more you communicate with someone, the more you see what's under the 'mask.' Cozy meals in a restaurant and quiet drinks in a pub where you can hear yourselves talk is one way to do this.

Direct open communication attracts the same, so it's important to be honest about whom you are and what your needs are and your date will hopefully do the same.

Try to build up a friendship with potential partners; all love that does not have true friendship for its base is like a mansion built on sand. The lust, the passion and the excitement of a new love affair always burns out. What have you got then if you do not have a friendship underneath?

Play' is important - laughing with each other, doing fun things like bowling, ice-skating and if you are really athletic try bungee jumping. Play will enable you to get to know each other, as when people are relaxed and having fun they don't need their masks. Play bypasses our defences.

You can discover more about a person in an hour of play
Than in a year of conversation.
Pluto

This theory does not only apply to potential partners, it applies to the friendships we attract too, it applies to every relationship we have in our lives.

It was interesting in my own life to watch a teenage family member (I will be in trouble if I mention his name) adapting his behavior and beliefs to 'fit in' with his peers. He was a sensible boy from a working class family who was lucky enough to get a scholarship to a private school.

He was there for two years and I watched him change from a grounded, down to earth boy to what I can only describe as a 'hooray Henry'. I felt that he became arrogant, judgmental and too big for his boots. His sense of dress became more eccentric and at this point in his life I did not like him very much. When I challenged him about this new behavior, he said that he needed to be like this to 'fit in'.

Remember that this was his belief; I know and have met some lovely boys that attend private school.

After two years he went to university and almost overnight he became a stereotypical student, he died his hair, wore sloppy dress, had fun nights out and I felt he became a much nicer character. It was amazing; it was like watching a chameleon changing colors' to blend in with his environment.

Recent research indicates that chameleon's do not change their colour for reasons of camouflage, but to indicate their mood, communicate and to <u>make themselves more attractive to potential mates.</u>

I will be in even more trouble if I mention that to him! However is that what we do? Are we all human chameleons that change our colour, our mask to fit in with others?

In friendships most of us can recall a situation in school when a friend that we trusted proved to be untrustworthy and told the world our inner most secrets, they let you down or maybe they pinched your boyfriend. It no doubt cut you like a knife. If it happened more than once, you probably started the creation of your masks. The 'you' that you will now only show to the world.

If you still wear those masks you are letting far too much of yesterday, use up today. Learn to let them go. Not everyone will betray your trust. To continue wearing this protective mask you are giving those that hurt you the power to change you.

We all come across those friends that we think are friends, but then we realize that we never feel good about ourselves when we are around them. So, what's the point of being around them?

These are not true friends. They are Frienimies. They try to make you feel bad about yourself to enable them to feel good about themselves. They will try to blow your candle out to make theirs shine brighter. Put your energy into the friendships that feel good to you.

Surround yourself with heart lifters, not heart sinkers

At one point in my own life I wondered why when people gave me critical feedback they gave it so bluntly, and yet with other's they were a little more sensitive. Some of this feedback devastated me at the time, it felt so cruel.

In time I recognised that it was because of the tough, strong mask that I wore. People thought that I could 'take it.' They did not need to be sensitive with me because they perceived that I could take harsh criticism and would not be greatly affected by it. Oh, but I was! The only problem was, I did not show it. I did not show my vulnerability. Is that my responsibility or there's? It's mine!

If I had taken off my 'tough cookie' mask then maybe they would have been a little more sensitive. I did not take off that tough cookie mask and the pain this caused me just helped me to create another mask to protect myself from hurt, from tough criticism which to me felt like a rejection. A cycle of masks that attracted more pain!

Every time you get hurt, laughed at, rejected, or abused a new mask or stronger old mask develops to hide the feelings, thoughts and behaviour that triggered that initial negative response.

I eventually learned to 'take the risk' and take off some of those masks and show my 'true self' - the outcome was extremely positive that I began to wonder why I had even wore those masks at all.

In families how many of you feel angry with your siblings because you seem to be the only one helping your elderly parents? Is this because of the 'mask' you wear "the helpful child.' Is it because your siblings think you want to do it all, so they take a step back? Have you told them that you need some help or do you say nothing and then build up resentments? Are we responsible for what happens to us because of the way that we present?

How do people see you in your own family? How would your friends describe you?

Ask them, it is an eye opener to hear how people you deem the closest to you, the ones that saw you grow up, the ones you thought would know you the best, don't really know you at all. That is because you have developed and been wearing these masks from a very young age. How many see your mask but don't actually see you?

Think of the relationships in your life that are currently in conflict.

- What are you presenting?

- What mask are you wearing?

- What thought or feeling are you hiding? Are you being authentic?

- What is it you are not saying?

Most of us think "why risk it" at least subconsciously. We are petrified of letting people see the 'bad stuff' in us. For fear of not being accepted. This is irrational thinking.

If you are being accepted by people because of the false front you present, then deep down you know that it is only the false front that is being accepted – **NOT THE REAL YOU!**

> "To be nothing but yourself in a world
> which is doing it's best, night and day,
> to make you everybody else -
> means to fight the hardest battle which
> any human being can fight;
> and never stop fighting."
> e.e. cummings

PERSONAL NOTES & EXERCISES:

Chapter Three
"Discovering your own masks"

ACCOMPLISHED

I'm very good at pretending to be me.
When I was little I dressed up in mom's or sometimes dad's clothes,
so I could pretend to be someone else.
Now I can't fit into anyone else's clothes
so instead I dress up in pseudo attitudes or moods.
Afraid to be seen naked.
Reluctant to look in the mirror in fear that
I'll catch a glimpse of the real me.
I wish that I could learn to swim,
to dive under the quilted blanket of sea greens and blues.
But the real me can't swim - won't swim,
in fear that I might drown.

Anita B - 1998 (Catharsis)

This chapter is aimed at helping you to discover the 'masks' that you wear. Don't forget that masks are created to protect us from pain. Discovering the character's that you have been playing in your life to protect you, can be a painful journey on its own.

Remember the masks are there for a reason and removing them involves taking a risk. Sometimes the masks help us to cope with childhood traumas such as abuse. If this were the case I would strongly advise that you seek therapy before attempting to risk removing these masks. They may be keeping you strong and safe for a reason. A therapist will help you to develop healthier coping strategies. (A Therapist can be found on the BACP website, on other counseling websites by typing 'local counsellor' in your search bar or through your GP).

Letting go of your masks can create a grieving process. There may be tears, but those tears are part of self-discovery. They are what help us to let go of the past and move into a healthier future. Your masks have become important to you, you may believe that they have protected you for most of your life, and they may have in lots of instances, but I would guess that in most instances they have created you more pain.

Sometimes we may need to keep them in storage just in case, and that's okay, because sometimes we may need them again for a short while.

You need to be sure that you are ready to do this and ensure that you feel safe in doing so. Find yourself some quiet time, where you will not be disturbed by the telephone or other distractions. This is something you can do either by yourself or with a close friend.

**Men cannot see their reflection in running water,
but only in still water. - Chuang Tzu**

The most important thing that I have learned on my own journey is to take 'safe risks' first. To show the 'real me' to the people I feel sure will not reject or hurt me; this empowers us to take bigger risks. Enjoy it can be fun!

There are some 'masks' that we know we wear and with

some contemplation we even know why we wear them. Other masks are much deeper in our unconsciousness and we may not be aware of them.

Take some time in thinking about the masks that you know you wear, and give those names of fictional characters.

This can either be television personalities, actors. pop stars, sports personalities, characters from a book or film. Write these names down and at the side of each one write down their personality traits, how you see their characters.

(Remember these are the 'Masks' we wear and not the 'Hats' we all may wear such as our 'mother' or 'wife' or 'professional' hats)

<u>Example:</u>

My 'Cagney' Mask	Strong, independent, tough (from Cagney and Lacey)
My 'Florence Nightingale' Mask	Caring, nurturing & calm
My 'Posh Spice' Mask	Classy & sophisticated

(Don't forget this will be how we perceive our 'characters' to be. Not everyone would agree).

Ask yourself the following questions:

- Where do you wear these masks?

- Who do you wear them with?

- How often?

- For how long have I worn this mask?

Now at the side of these characters/masks write down:

- What part of 'me' do they hide?

<u>Example:</u>

My 'Cagney' Mask	hides	My needy self
My 'Florence' Mask	hides	My angry self
My 'Posh' Mask	hides	My scruffy self

Now take some time to think about why we don't show the hidden side to others:

- What might happen?

- What do we fear?

- Do we have any evidence to back up those fears?

- Did showing that side of you cause you some pain in the past?

- If so where's the evidence that this will happen in the present or in the future?

Think about a person/relationship from the past that has caused you pain:

- Was it because they had only seen the 'mask?'

- Had they been attracted to you by the mask?

- Was it your responsibility because you only showed them the mask?

People who have only seen the 'mask' are confused when you show them the 'real you,' as this was not how they originally perceived you.

Imagine that a friend had only seen 'Posh Spice,' then you went through a period of feeling low and could not be bothered to dress or do your hair and make- up.

This could throw him/her. S/he may not know how to deal with the 'scruffy you.' S/hes perceived you as usually always so strong, so immaculately turned out. Unfortunately when some people don't know how to handle things, they often walk away, and they can have a need to distance themselves from you. This is more about them than you.

So, this friend can't wait to get away from you because s/he's never seen you like this before, s/he does not know what to say. So s/he makes an excuse to leave. You may then perceive this as rejection, this then reinforces your beliefs that you are rejected for being low, depressed, scruffy and therefore the 'Posh spice' mask is reinforced. Your belief that it is not okay to be scruffy or low around him/her, or maybe anyone has been further heightened! Don't let their rejection of you create even bigger defenses.

Of course most true friendships would be far more accepting if you had a 'scruffy or weak day.' but imagine if this person had a dislike of needy people due to their own past experiences and liked you because you were strong and independent. Don't forget it was 'Cagney' or 'Posh' that attracted this person to you, maybe because they were quite needy and valued your strength in the relationship. So when you became needy and vulnerable yourself and needed their support they were unable to be there for you.

We have to be accountable for the way that we present ourselves to others and accept that the things that may happen to us when we 'show our true selves' is because we were not fully honest at the beginning of the relationship. However, it is important to remember that 'true and genuine friends' will accept this 'different you'. Freinimies often won't or can't.

We often attract people for what we offer. If we offer strength and then they see you weak, a frenimie will no longer have any use for you, a friend will support you when you need them too.

Don't be afraid of sharing your vulnerabilities – your fear, envy, frustration. It will make you realize how alike we all are. You will be amazed to hear again and again 'Yeah, me, too!'
Source unknown

Look back at your masks and ask yourself:

- Are your masks helpful?

- Are there times in your life when they have been helpful/ unhelpful?

- Have they caused you to be misunderstood?

- Treated badly?

- Have they attracted people into your life to later discover that they liked you for your mask not for who you really are?

Spend some time exploring the above. If you like writing, try writing all this down in a journal, it will help you to reflect. This type of exploration will help your emotional growth.

I often find clients say *"I don't know who the real 'me' is anymore.'* Sometimes this is because they have spent so long being whom they thought others wanted them to be, that they have lost sight of who they really are.

If this sounds like you, try this exercise:

Spend a couple of minutes thinking about

- Who was your hero as a child.
- Who was it you thought *"I want to be like him/her when I grow up."*

It is usually a TV personality, actor, a singer, a sports star or a character from a book or film or maybe a teacher or a family member. Write down the first name that comes into your head.

Now write down five or six strong characteristics of this person (not what they looked like). Describe their personality.

For example:

Cagney: *Strong, independent, sexy, fiery, stubborn, energetic.*

DON'T READ ON UNTIL YOU HAVE DONE THIS!

Now read through that list and describe yourself. The 'self' that others see you as. Was there a connection? Occasionally there is not, but in most cases when you have described your hero you have described yourself, and how you present when describing the six strong characteristics of your hero.

If that's what you have done, described yourself. Isn't that amazing? So how come you have the same personality/characteristics as your hero?

Try it on a few friends you will be amazed at how many choose a character that is very much like them self   i.e. the 'self' that they present to the world, even you.

You may ask yourself then, 'as we grow do we take on the personalities of our hero's?' I believe out of awareness we do.

Our hero's are often chosen because they have the personality traits that we admire and think we need to protect ourselves from pain. They often have characteristics that we envy and wish we had ourselves.

Remember this is on an unconscious level and what this exercise does is bring this into your conscious awareness.

So if this is the 'you' that you are presenting, let's look at the 'real you'.

Next to your hero's characteristics write down the opposite meanings, i.e:

CAGNEY	ME
Strong	*Weak/Vulnerable*
Independent	*Dependent*
Sexy	*Loving*
Fiery	*Calm*
Compromising	*Stubborn*
Energetic	*Tired*
Cold	*Warm*

You may be able to add more to your lists. What do you notice?

In most cases we are hiding all the things that are 'human,' all the things that we fear showing and perhaps all the things that we have received negative responses to in the past. We are hiding all the things that we have developed our masks to hide.

It is okay to be weak, vulnerable, dependent, loving, calm, compromising and tired. **It is okay to 'be you!'**

Now look at those two character lists and imagine they are two people stood in front of you.

- Which one would you like best?

- Which one would you feel more comfortable with?

- Which one would you feel that you can be your 'real self' with?

- Which one would you feel inadequate, weak or inferior to?

Ironically most people will choose 'the real person.' Why then do we wear those masks? They do not represent the 'real' you, they can create dislike and they can make people feel uncomfortable with you.

Wouldn't you much prefer to be liked and accepted for who you really are?

Think about how the mask you wear makes other people feel. Could these 'feelings' set you up for further pain or rejection?

Now think about how the 'real you' makes other people feel. Could these 'feelings' set you up for pain or rejection?

This above all: to thine own self be true
William Shakespheare

I can recall a friend who had known me for eight years reading a journal I had written at the time, it was when I was first on my journey of discovering the 'real me.' In this journal I wrote all about the real me. The 'me' that I did not show to others. It was risky. I was scared about what she might think of my vulnerabilities. I imagined that she might not like the 'weak me' - and even worse reject me or abuse my vulnerabilities. I had, I hasten to add no evidence to support this.

I pottered around making coffee with knots of anxiety in my stomach. When she had finished there were tears in her eyes and she said,

"Linda, I like this person! Much better than the person you present. The 'real you' enables me to feel human"

I asked her to expand on this as it would help my own personal growth. She said:

"The 'you' I have known for eight years, the strong, indestructible, always together 'you' makes me feel inadequate because I can't be like you. It makes me feel ashamed of my own vulnerabilities. When something happens and I crumble I feel weak when I compare myself to how you manage pain"

Little did she know that I did crumble, but inside, in privacy. She continued,

"Now I can see that like me, you feel pain, you feel hurt and sometimes you are not so tough. I can see that 'cut you and you bleed' before I could not see these things. Seeing you as a human being helps me to see myself as a human being too."

Some of us I guess bleed internally and some of us bleed externally. I did not want my friend to feel that she was a 'hot mess' in a crisis and feel inadequate because I wasn't. The truth was that I could be a 'hot mess' too at times, but I was a 'hot mess' in private.

My fantasies that she might reject or abuse me were unfounded. The 'tough cookie' mask that I wore so adeptly affected her beliefs about herself, and subsequently had an impact on the mask she chose to wear with me!

In the eight years of our friendship neither of us was being authentic; neither of us really knew the other intimately. How many years would we have continued pretending if she had not read my 'real me' journal.

It's interesting I think to come to the realisation of how our masks affect other people's beliefs. Would we intentionally want them to feel weak and inadequate? I don't think so, and yet we can do.

So, acceptance of our self and being able to be our true self enables others to be more accepting of themselves too. This is a great gift that we can give to our friends?

**Acceptance of others, their looks, their behaviours, their beliefs,
bring you an inner peace and tranquillity
- instead of anger and resentment.
Source unknown**

It may be interesting for you to look back at exercise two and three and the masks that you have developed and think about the effect that they may have on other people.

- When you wear your mask what reaction do you arouse in others?

- Is there a pattern of any kind in your relationships?

Now look at your own mask and answer the same questions. What did you discover?

Now look at the two characters' I earlier described:

'Cagney' and 'Me.'

- Look back at 'Cagney's personality traits.

- What type of person would you imagine 'Cagney' to attract?

- Would she attract a giving person or would a giving person look at her and say "What have I got to give this person, she appears to have everything"

- Could she be scaring off potential suitors?

CAGNEY

The mask	The type of person this mask may attract
Strong	*A needy person?*
Independent	*A dependent person?*
Sexy	*A highly sexed person?*
Fiery	*An argumentative person?*
Stubborn	*A moody person*
Energetic	*A lively person*

We know that the above is a mask. Is that the type of person that the 'real' character would connect with do you think? Let's look at the type of person the 'real' person might attract:

ME

The real person	The person 'I' might attract
Weak	*A strong person?*
Dependant	*A supportive person?*
Warm	*An affectionate person?*
Calm	*A peaceful person?*
Compromising	*Understanding person?*
Tired	*A helpful person?*

I know which person I would rather be around and that is the person 'ME' attracts. What about you?

Now try doing the same with your own characters and the 'real you'.

Is it any wonder then that relationships breakdown? Is it surprising then that we attract the opposite to what we want? It's almost like faking an orgasm. How can we get what we need if we don't say what we need or if we present in a way that attracts the opposite to what we need. And how can we be disappointed in the results we get when this is the way we present ourselves?

I did exercise three 'who was your hero?' on a friend of mine who was showing an interest in my counseling training at the time. Without any hesitation she said

"Doris Day" When asking her to briefly describe her character, she said,

"Oh, she was just so perfect! She was always the perfect housewife, the perfect mother, the perfect schoolteacher. Every role she played she was perfect, there was never a hair out of place and her clothes and make-up were always immaculate"

I looked at my friend in astonishment, because she had just described herself to a tee!

I had often felt inadequate alongside her - she had five young children, a large home and a husband - and yet no matter what time of the day you walked into her home, it was always immaculate. She was always immaculate, and the kids were always immaculate! When she opened a cupboard in the kitchen, everything was smartly laid out - even her baked bean tins were polished for Christ's sake! It made me feel like an utter slob, and reinforced my own 'worthless' beliefs.

These beliefs left me with negative feelings about myself. I would return home not feeling very good about myself.

The problem with not feeling good about yourself is that you then start behaving in a different more negative way. For example: snapping at others, isolating others, drinking excessively etc. These behaviours then reinforce those negative beliefs and a cycle begins.

However when changing the belief to "It's okay to be untidy, we're not all the same," my feelings and behaviour would change.

Interesting enough when I asked her who she would like to be, she said "a slob." The poor girl was always tired, always searching for something exciting to happen in her life, stressed and frustrated with life. She would have 'burn outs' frequently from trying to keep on top of everything. These 'burn outs' would trigger massive rows with her partner, which would then make her try even harder to be perfect.

Her values appeared to be around 'being a good housewife' & 'looking good' - to be accepted. I liked her, and would have liked her just as much, if not more if she were 'a slob' occasionally.

This exercise made her look at a new way of 'being' and she became more laid back about things. It enabled her to have more energy to do the things she wanted to do with her life. She made fresh decisions about whom and where she wanted to be. She began to see that if people only like her because she was 'perfect' then this were not a genuine like.

Genuine people like you for whoever or whatever you are.

It is astounding how many people can become involved with Mental Health professionals after years of trying to be 'perfect' or 'strong' trying to be who they believe they 'should'be. It is mentally draining for them trying to be who they think others want them to be, until eventually it becomes too much! I have lost count of clients who really believed that they needed to be this 'type of person' to be loved and accepted by others.

It becomes such an enlightenment for them when they realize what they have been doing and that they don't have to 'be this phony person' anymore. It is a pleasure to see the changes when they start to believe and accept that they are great people as they are.

Dropping those masks, those defenses that we have been carrying around for many years is refreshing, it enables us to do the things that we want to do, that we are capable of doing. We have the energy to achieve; we are not tied down with anger, resentment, depression, anxiety, and stress. We can just 'be'.

You cannot change your destination overnight,
But you can change your direction overnight!
Source unknown

This is another exercise you may like to try, particularly if exercise two and three did not work for you

If you were to describe yourself as a container, which container would it be?

1. Imagine you are a container which container would you be?

2. How useful am I?

3. How do I feel as the container?

4. What do people do with me?

5. How do you see yourself?

6. How do you think others see you?

7. Would you like to change?

8. Where do I belong?

9. Given a free choice what container would you choose to be and why?

This exercise might help you to recognise what you do or be for others rather than yourself and who you want to be. Be the container you want to be, that's important for your own well-being.

One of the most popular masks that people tend to wear in our society is the 'Miss goody two shoes' mask', the people pleaser, the one that avoids confrontation no matter what. How true are these people being to themselves?

It is okay to say 'No'. It is okay to confront something that you are not happy about. If you don't then without a doubt the anger and bitterness will come back at a later date and bite you on the bum, usually at a time that you least expect it.

Try writing a 'real you' journal, you may be surprised at what you discover. You could write in your journal the type of 'people' you would like in your life. This will help you to attract them.

So is now the time to start being the 'real you?' For how many more years will you continue to be who you think other people want you to be? How many more people are you going to 'impress' or 'annoy' or have an adverse affect on by being the 'phony' you!

For how much longer do you intend to try and captivate people with the mask that you wear and then find that when they get to know the 'real you' you are not compatible.

What you are doing when you wear these masks is lying to yourself. A lie is something that you make yourself believe in order to make life a little easier. A lie is a paradigm under which you operate to avoid pain. A lie will destroy you, inside and out. A lie is a something you want to believe because to consider the opposite would hurt your ego. A lie sucks you into relationships with the wrong people, people that you are not compatible with. The truth will draw more compatible people to you.

In the next chapter we will learn about the choices we make in life for others, and in further chapters we will explore the experiences that 'change' us from being who we want to be.

As I have previously said showing your 'real self' is scary, it is a journey into the unknown; it is about developing new behaviours and new beliefs.

Let me warn you it is not an easy task. It takes time and patience. It can feel harder sometimes surviving without our masks, but in the long run you will feel much better.

Time and time again I see people who when making these changes their life becomes much more enjoyable.

Throwing out the old and bringing in the new can be difficult when you have held on to these behaviours/beliefs for years. But, change only happens when we are ready, no amount of therapy or self-help books can make you change, <u>you have to want to change</u>. And change can feel uncomfortable at first.

A colleague once asked me to put my watch on my other arm. I curiously did as he asked. He then asked me how that felt and I truthfully told him that it felt uncomfortable, weird, and not quite right. I was not used to wearing my watch on this arm.

He said **"That's what change is like Linda."**

He then requested that I leave my watch on the 'wrong' arm for a week. I did as he asked and I soon forgot it was there. He collared me, a week later, and asked what my watch felt like now.

I replied "Okay, good it would be strange putting it on my other arm now"

He said **"That's what change is like"** and left me to ponder that thought. It may feel strange, but the longer you persist, the stranger your **old** beliefs and behaviours and ways of being will become. The new ones will feel more normal.

Change happens when we feel safe; our bodies often have a way of stopping us from looking at things we are not ready to look at. Change happens sometimes when we are at our lowest, or when we find that we are feeling 'stuck' or stagnated in our lives.

Are you ready to wear purple with a red hat and pink slippers and blow gum bubbles in the middle of Asda without fears of re-experiencing early experiences that were painful?

Not yet, that's okay. Read on.

Working towards change

**"And then the time came, when the risk to
remain tight in a bud,
was more painful, than the risk it took to bloom!"
Source unknown**

PERSONAL NOTES AND EXERCISES:

Chapter Four

"Choices"

ON A TIRED HOUSEWIFE

Here lies a poor housewife who was always tired.
She lived in a house where help was not hired;
Her last words on earth were: "Dear friends, I am going
To where there's no cooking, or washing, or sewing.
For everything there is exact to my wishes,
For where they don't eat there's no washing of dishes.
I'll be where loud anthems will always be ringing,
But having no voice I'll be quit of the singing.
Don't mourn for me now, don't mourn for me never,
I'm going to do nothing for ever and ever!

ANON

Why did this poor lady feel that she had to wait until she died to have peace in her life, to stop most probably being the 'perfect housewife?'

It is okay to be a good housewife of course, if that's what you want to be. If this is the real you. Equally it is okay to be a 'good enough' housewife. Some of us choose that way of life and that's okay, but how many of us do it because it is expected of us? I'm not suggesting that you 'do nothing forever and ever,' just that you spend more time doing or at least thinking about doing more of what you would like to do.

I am giving you permission and the freedom to leap beyond the boundaries of fear and anxiety and 'be' the person that you want to be!

To jump from one cliff to another (the unknown) can be risky, but think about the times you have done it, usually something positive always comes from taking this risk. How many of us are in jobs that we don't enjoy, because we are scared of change? Or it's the career path our parents wanted us to take? Or how many of us conform to what we think our parents/caretakers, partners, friends, employers want us to be?

Carrying those beliefs can have a huge impact on your future life script.

For most of the time we do not 'check out' the evidence. Remember "WE THINK" they want us to be. <u>Most of the time people just want us to be happy and to be ourselves.</u>

If we were given a choice of life scripts when we were born would we have chosen the one that we are now living? It is never too late to change your script or a character that you are playing, that you no longer want to play. It is never too late to get rid of a few of those masks. It is never too late to do the things we want to do, and it is never too late to be you!

Have a go at writing a script, a story of how you want the rest of your life to be, or even how you want the next month to be.

Example

> *"Next year I am going to college to take up art classes. I will meet like-minded people. I will be as spontaneous and genuine as I can in my relationships. I will take the risk at my next appraisal at work and ask my boss for a rise. I will tell him why I think I deserve it.*
>
> *Next time I am spoken to in a nasty way I will tell the person how it affects me and how I would like to be spoken to. I will also wear more funky gear and not worry about what people think."*

If you do 'one' of those things, you have begun to change your 'life script.'

Make not your thoughts your prisons
William Shakespeare

Some therapists may ask you to think about your 'death bed scene' and if given the choice what would you have done differently. I am going to ask you to imagine the same scene but ask you 'who would you be?'

The mask you described earlier in this book (in chapter three) or the 'real you.'

You don't get to choose how you're going to die. Or when.
You can only decide how you're going to live. Now.
Source unknown

If you are the real you, how might your life be

different? Take some time to think about this. Write down your thoughts.

If you are finding this difficult, after all who wants to think about the end of their life? Try this:

Think of a fairy tale character or a character from a book or someone from history that best describes you. Now write a little about the characteristics and story of this person, i.e:

Cinderella: Hard working, always sad, never does anything romantic or exciting, never does anything that she enjoys or for herself. She suffers in silence, is bullied by others. She mostly feels tired and lethargic.

Now describe a similar character that you would like to be:

Lady Diana: Warm, compassionate, vulnerable and is not frightened of showing her weaknesses. She is kind and empathic, spiritual, angry and risk taking.

(Remember these characters are how you see them, not everyone will see them in the same way).

So, what's stopping you from being the character that you would like to be? Is this character more like the true you? Why wait until you are too old to be who you want to be, to be who you really are, to wear purple.

Be careful that you do not swap one mask for another mask, check out that the character you feel more comfortable with is the one that is nearer to the 'real you'.

How many times have you said or have you heard people say "I would love to give painting, acting, writing, singing, flower arranging etc a go" and when asked why they don't. They usually say, "I haven't got the time." If you think about it when we are born to the day that we leave this earth we are given plenty of time. It is down to us what we choose to do with that time. We learn from a young age how to manage money but do we ever learn how to manage time? Is time more important to you than money?

The energy it takes being who you think others want you to be, does not give you the time or energy to do the things that you want to do.

Be you and you will be taken aback by how much time you have!

It's not just the masks we wear; it's the pain that we often get from wearing those masks or the resentments we build up 'being' for other people, which sap us of this energy.

How many times have you experienced emotional pain and spent hours and hours re-running the event through your head?

I should have ……….. Why does this always happen to me…………… If only..…………. Next time I will…………..

Or thinking of ways in which you can pay the person back who has hurt you. Think of what else you could have done with that time. Holding on to anger and resentments is like holding on to a hot coal, the only one to get burned is you.

Wasted psychological energy depletes us of our physical energy!

I shall wear purple

My friend was brought a paint easel, paints and canvasses by her husband because she said she wanted to paint. Two years later she still had not started, when I asked her why she said "because I haven't got the time," She was retired and had loads of free time. When I challenged this she said "what if I am not very good at it." The 'time excuse' was an unauthentic comment. Her real reason came out when she was challenged.

When I convinced her that it did not matter, she began to paint and now most of her friends (including myself) have one of her paintings up on their wall. They're good! How would she have known if she had not tried? Her belief, anxiety and fear that she would not be very good at it, could have held her back and stopped her from enjoying this now lucrative hobby.

Is it time for you to look at how much psychological energy you waste?

While writing this book, another friend asked what my book was about, and as usual it always opens up a conversation, sets people thinking about their own lives. This friend is the complete opposite to the one I described earlier (Doris Day)).

This one does not make housework her priority. However, it irritates her when her sister comes round and criticizes her housekeeping; she asked me why I thought her house being a mess bothered her sister so much?

I felt that it might be because "Being a good housewife' is her sister's belief of what she needs to be to feel accepted. She may have a 'be perfect' mask. If this was the 'real her' it would not bother her how other people lived.

Once you have accepted yourself and your own flaws, then you are able to accept other people and their flaws.

If her belief system is that "you won't be accepted/loved/liked if you live in chaos," she will believe the same for my friend. "Tidy your house or what will people think of you" is possibly her perception. The ironic thing is 'everyone' loves this friend; she is such fun to be around. We don't look at her house and to me it is quite nice and homely.

This same friend disclosed that she loves 'swings' and when she is on one she feels 'free' - the higher she goes the freer she feels - it enables her to de-stress, however she never goes on one unless she takes children to the park. The children give her an excuse to go on a swing.

Please go to the park and go on a swing mate, if that's what you want to do, do it!

Now for you:

- How many things do you choose not to do or do you do because of what people might think?

- How much of your life is controlled by others?

That is not to suggest that we all go out and rob a bank right this minute, because we all know the consequences of that behaviour. The consequences of certain behaviour's can create bigger problems. But what are the consequences of going to the park and going on a swing?

What are the consequences of leaving the housework?

What are the consequences of taking off your masks and showing the real you? Are the consequences 'real' or are they fantasies? Is it your own internal belief system because of messages you receive from others or from personal experiences?

I shall wear purple

A client I was working with presented to me with stress. He said that the ethos of the organisation that he worked for was very competitive and the expectation was to work hard.

To enable him to keep up with this, even his spare time was taken up with thoughts of work. I explained to him that while you're thinking about work, you're doing it! He therefore did not appear to have any 'switch off' time.

He was being who he thought his employers wanted him to be. He had a very strong belief that if he did not continue at this pace, he might lose his job and that someone better might take his place. The reality was that if he continued 'at this pace' he probably would lose his job. He was 'setting himself up,' out of awareness for his own fantasy to come true.

While working with this client we explored the origin of his beliefs and discovered that he had developed this belief from several negative experiences in his life resulting in him wearing 'people pleasing' and 'try hard' masks. I could see that these masks were a hindrance and actually likely to set him up for his biggest fear.

We reality tested his need for these masks and explored what he feared most about removing them. He discovered that what he feared most was almost happening in his life. He eventually took the risk of being 'himself' at work and did what he could, without busting a gut. He came to me and said

"It's strange really Linda, because I actually get more done now and make fewer mistakes, and my boss has even commented on my performance, something he has never done before"

When he stopped trying so hard to please, he actually had more energy to 'do'. When he stopped thinking about work at the weekend he went to work on Monday fresh and with more energy.

**If you change the way you look at things,
The things you look at change!**

Have you noticed that people working shifts are more tired than those in a nine to five job? If you are on for example a 'two till ten shift' half your morning is spent preparing for and thinking about work. If this is you, then try and get into a pattern of not thinking about work until an hour before you are due to go. After-all most people only get up an hour before work.

Another mask that work conscientious people wear is the "Perfectionist" - they have a need for their work to be perfect. Who can ever be perfect, this is near impossible. We all make mistakes and we learn more from our mistakes than our successes and often those that try so hard to be perfect make more mistakes than the rest of us.

If this is you, stop setting yourself up for failure. Trying so hard to be perfect is a sure way of failing. We are only mere human beings it is impossible for us to be perfect. Please be happy with just 'being good enough'. If you do not then you will always be disappointed in yourself!

We all know someone like this, the person who when given constructive criticism takes it to heart because what we are saying to that person is that 'you are not perfect' - this is a battle for this type of person because when their belief is 'I must be perfect' you are in fact challenging their belief system. You are telling them they are 'not' what they believe that they must be.

How much time do you spend thinking about work out of work hours? Is this the change you might like to make in your life? How much quality time do you give yourself? How much relaxation time do you allow yourself?

What I'd like you to do now is divide a large sheet of paper into two columns.

Write at the top of the first column what you believe you have to do, and on the second, what you would choose to do given a choice, i.e:

WHAT I HAVE TO DO	WHAT I CHOOSE TO DO
The housework	Go for a walk in the park
Be good at my job	Be just good enough
Look good all the time	Slob out all day and write a book or journal
Clean the car	Go for a facial
Be happy all the time	Show my true feelings
Do the washing and ironing	Go swimming
Don't get too close to people	Let my friend know she hurt me
Do the shopping	Go on a swing
Cook meals	Eat out
Never cry	Let my partner know what I need
Be an adult all the time	Have some childish fun
Be a tough cookie	Show my vulnerability to just one person
Do everything myself	Delegate and ask someone to do something for you

- Look at your first list. (What I have to do):

- How many of these things do you really 'have to' do?

- What will happen if you don't?

- Where's your evidence that something bad/negative will happen?

My guess is at least half of these things are not necessary, and that nothing drastic is going to happen if you don't do them and please remember it is okay to have a good cry, crying is a release of pent up emotion and why would you want to hang on to pent up emotion?

Now cross some of those off the first list that you have now realised you don't 'have to' do and do some of the things on the second list!

WOW! Now you have got some more time for you. Well done!

It may feel risky at first but the more you do this the easier it becomes. Let's face it, who is going to die if you don't do the washing and the ironing? What is the worst that can happen if you go on a swing? And let out those tears they are healing, and did you know the saltier they are the deeper the pain. Pain you have been hanging on to, for what reason? Let them out, why would you want to store up your pain. I have a motto "**Feel it to heal it.**"

Now I'd like you to write a list of who you don't want to be and who you do want to be:

Column A   Column B

Don't want to be:	Do want to be:
So blooming perfect	More laid back
So strong	Show my weaknesses
Try so hard	More chilled
In such a rush	Slower
A people pleaser	More assertive

Now create a column in the middle headed "What I need to do to get from column A to B": The column in the middle needs to read the things you need to do to change. Don't panic we are just writing these things down for the minute. Then of course, it is always your choice if you want to change these things.

Column A   What I need   Column B
                  to do?

Don't want to be:		Do want to be:
So blooming perfect	Explore what might happen if I get things wrong. If other people get things wrong, count to ten before reacting. If something isn't perfect, ask yourself in the scheme of	Be more laid back

	things how important is it? Give myself permission to get things wrong. Laugh at myself more. Be more accepting of mine and other's imperfections. Allow myself to be 'just good enough!	

Enjoy! You have just made a choice. A choice that is not ruled by others, or what you believe others expect of you. Well done!

Each time you behave in the way that you don't want to behave, remember that this is a mask that you wear to protect yourself from pain. It was a mask that you developed at an age when you did not know what else to do, when your resources were limited.

It was at a time when you felt that you needed to 'be this character' to protect yourself. You are an adult now, you can make another decision you can decide to be who you want to be, if you want to be more laid back, be more laid back.

What is the risk? There is no risk!

I have recently given up a well paid job to write this book, to take a break and do some of the things on my 'what I choose to do list.' It was not an easy decision; it was in fact quite scary, jumping off a comfortable, secure place into the unknown. I don't know at this point if it will ever be published, but what I do know is that it is something I wanted to try. (If you are reading this then YEH I have been published!)

I knew the timing was right, I knew this because I never felt any intense anxiety once the decision had been taken. In my experience your body tells you if you are doing the right thing, and when the time is right.

Learn to listen to your body more, we have two processes going on 'the thought process' and 'the feeling process' - the thought process is great for reality testing, logical thinking and analysing, but if you need to make an important decision, listen to the feeling content too because that will tell you of the psychological and emotional impact that any decision will have on your life.

Most people will only listen to one of these processes and that's when we make decisions that are not always the right one. To make an important decision in your life or to make changes ask yourself. What are my thoughts telling me to do? What are my feelings telling me to do? Which of these are the strongest?

I am a contradiction, a perfect imperfection,
On looking in from outside, I think I'd pass inspection.
My nails are neat, each hair in place, my clothes the latest
styles
But look a little closer, and you can see my trials.

My best intentions lead to pain, and complicated messes,
My head is filled with wishes, my decisions second guesses.
There was a time I tried to hide each wrinkle, scar and tear,
But I'm learning to appreciate, that I'm more than I appear.
Each wrinkle tells a story, the path from there to here,
I've earned a little wisdom, with every falling tear.
Perhaps I'll let my hair go wild, and skip the manicure,
I'll wear my favourite colour, they'll say "Hey, look at her"

My hair, my heart, my clothes, my soul,

Will walk in one direction.
No longer contradicting
My perfect imperfection!

Mellissa Bachara - 2005 (adapted)

PERSONAL NOTES AND EXERCISES:

Chapter Five

"Self Esteem"

BEING WHO WE ARE

How many games do we play
When we don't know who to be
And how many masks do we wear
When we are blind and cannot see?

Just be myself and who I am
Or so the mentors say
Stand straight and tall to face the world
In the rising of each new day

Will my weakness show, will they all see
The insecurities I hide behind
Will my fears be known, my flaws exposed
With the doubts lurking in my mind?

Or do I take that giant leap
To prove my worthiness
By presenting the me I carry inside
With humbling grace and modest finesse?
Please accept me just the way I am
Someone better no less than you
And together we can remove our masks

As we start our lives anew~ StinaLisa~

Why is it that we can't bear the thought of people seeing us as we really are? It is usually because we do not like who we really are. Before we can allow others to see the inner parts of us, we have to firstly accept our self.

Accepting who you are and what you are capable of will help you to let go of the masks that are protecting your vulnerabilities, the masks that are protecting you from past hurts and fears. When you accept yourself unconditionally you will learn how to trust again, you will have the confidence in others to let down your 'strong' mask and show your weaknesses.

Self-acceptance is being happy and loving with who you are, even those parts of ourselves that we would eventually like to change. If we are not comfortable with ourselves we will always hide behind our masks.

Behind each mask is our true face - the face that, for whatever reason, we are afraid to show to others. With our mask, we portray confidence, happiness, strength, friendliness all the things that we think others want from us and all the things that we think that we like in others. Yet underneath all of this we are often struggling with our own perceived inadequacies. That is all of us, every man and every woman that you know.

Lord forbid if the mask should slip, allowing others to see the real us! What would they think if they saw the face behind our mask? Would they be disappointed to see the imperfections that we work so hard to hide? Or would they be relieved to know that we are more alike than they may have thought.

If we were all our true selves, and none of us hid behind our masks then it would be easier to accept each other's and our own inadequacies or faults as we could then see that we were all human.

However, our fears keep the mask in place. We go through life never really getting to know each other past the surface of our masks. Attempting to be what we think others want. Remember the friend I talked about earlier in the book, the one that I had known for eight years. We never got to know each other in eight years beyond the surface of our masks. How sad is that?

The mask becomes a part of us, but if we can't let down the mask once in a while, no one will ever see us - the whole of us. And in our heart of hearts, isn't that what we really want - another person to accept the whole of us?

The best part of living without a mask is that we get to experience true acceptance.

When I get a compliment, for being 'ME' not for my mask it is the greatest compliment of all. When you let someone get to know you **'the real you'** and they accept you, you will feel appreciated in a way that you have never felt when wearing your masks.

The mask is a part of our personality that we artificially identify with and show the world on an unconscious level. The mask is who we think we should be or wish we could be, how we want others to perceive us, and it is all based on our idealized self-image. Hence, why we become 'our hero's' and wear our hero's personalities/characteristics.

If we're suffering from low self-esteem, we try to hide the fact as best we can, using the masks we've created, or, as some may put it, "going through our act." "I am the perfect wife." "I am cool, calm and strong." These are all part of the manifestation of the 'false self' that we have created.

The lower our self esteem the more masks we appear to wear. After all if we don't like ourselves then how can we expect others to like us, so we begin to create masks to hide behind, to hide the parts of ourselves that we dislike? The more parts of 'us' that we dislike, the more masks we will develop.

However, <u>YOU</u> are unique. A large percentage of our personal view of 'self' is said to be based on what we think others think of us.

Therefore, our self-concept is based on the fickleness of other people's opinions!?

To accept and love yourself is to place no conditions on yourself on how you 'should' behave. It is about taking a risk and being open and vulnerable to whom you are. Once you accept yourself you will realise that there is no need to wear a mask or act in a way just to please other people. You will be able to recognise that it is okay to be vulnerable and that this supports your ability to have open and honest relationships with others.

If you do not give yourself unconditional self acceptance you will feel the need to act in ways which go against your own beliefs and feelings, you will lack the freedom to be yourself. This in itself can create all types of psychological ailments and an inability to relax.

Remember what I said earlier about the 'key in the front door.' If you come in after a night out and put the key in the front door and feel a sense of relief, feel your shoulders drop and begin to feel relaxed, then that will tell you that for most or all of

the day/evening you have been wearing your masks.

If you do not accept yourself unconditionally, you will spend most of your life pleasing other people instead of pleasing yourself. You may strive to be perfect in everything that you do, setting yourself up for continuous failures as it is impossible to be perfect, which in turn will lower your self esteem as you will never feel 'good enough'.

You may spend a good part of your life being defensive and struggling with relationships or isolate yourself from other people to protect yourself, creating quite a lonely lifestyle. You may suppress anger which will fester away inside of you building up resentments. You may not show that you have been hurt again holding those feelings inside. What happens to those feelings?

They come back periodically to bite you on the bum. They deplete you of psychological and physical energy. They manifest into psychological problems such as stress, anxiety, depression. They can manifest into physical symptoms such as IBS, headaches, skin problems and many more.

Why would you want to do all of this to yourself?

We wear masks as a part of a survival mechanism, but they can often create more wounds then they aim to protect. They become deeply destructive and do not help us to survive.

Ask yourself the following questions:

- How often do you wear a mask?

- With whom?

- What are some of the things that you hide behind a mask?

- How does wearing a mask help or hinder your self esteem?

- What things do you need to do or be in order to be accepted?

Low self esteem is destructive. It can contribute to our fear of rejection, causing us to avoid getting close to people (showing our 'real self'). It can leave us with feelings of sadness, anxiety, guilt, shame, humiliation, frustration and anger. It can keep us from communicating our true feelings and keep us isolated and unable to be vulnerable.

How many masks would you guess one would need to then wear to hide all those downbeat feelings, if they are not acceptable feelings to show or express for you?

Sadness requires a happy mask; can any of us be happy all of the time? How much energy would that take?

Self esteem is the opinion you have of yourself. You can't touch it, but it effects how you feel. You can't see it, but it's there when you look in the mirror. You can't hear it, but it is there every time you talk about yourself.

Having a high self esteem is not boasting about how great you are. It is more like quietly knowing that you are worth a lot, priceless in fact. It is not about thinking you are perfect – because nobody is – but knowing that you are worthy of being loved and accepted. Nor is self esteem like a new dress or shirt that you'd love to have, but don't have. Everyone needs to have self esteem.

A good self esteem is important. It helps you to hold your head up high and feel proud of yourself. It gives you the courage to try new things and the power to believe in yourself. It empowers you to make changes in your life, reach goals and respect yourself, and it enables you to let go of those phony masks that you are wearing.

The 'real you' is okay, the 'real you' is acceptable and loveable.

The real you is unique. There will never be another you, you and your life is precious. If we are given something precious we look after it, we value it, we speak highly of it to our friends, and we love it. You are precious so therefore need to speak highly of yourself, look after yourself and value yourself.

People with high self esteem are able to accept and learn from their own mistakes. They are confident without being obnoxious or conceited and not devastated by criticism. They are not overly worried about failing or looking neither foolish nor easily defeated by setbacks and obstacles. They do not feel the need to put others down or are they destructively critical of themselves.

We talked earlier in the book about friends/partners and relations, anyone in your life that puts you down are possibly suffering from a very low self esteem themselves. My answer to those people is always "You know honey, you don't have to blow my candle out to shine brighter, yours shines pretty bright itself" - I am letting them know in a sensitive way what they are doing and also reminding them of their own unique qualities.

People with a high self esteem tend to be open and assertive and have the ability to laugh at themselves. They wear very few masks. The lower your self esteem, the less you think of yourself and accept yourself. This will help you to create more masks and then no-one will know who you really are and no-one will accept you for you!

So start raising your self esteem today.......... by:

Loving and accepting yourself, if you can do this then you can accept that you are human and subsequently accept that to make mistakes <u>is</u> human. Celebrating your strengths and achievements, forgiving yourself for your mistakes and not dwelling on your weaknesses, every human being has them.

Change the way that you talk to yourself and stop putting yourself down. Do not judge yourself against unreasonable expectations and stop beating yourself up for your weaknesses.

You cannot change your past, but you can change the way you see yourself today.

Make a LONG list of all the good things you have done. If you catch yourself saying nasty things to yourself STOP! Recite your list of achievements to yourself.

Convince yourself to be proud of what you have done. STOP bullying yourself, if you hit anyone with a 'big stick' it is bound to decrease their self esteem, so why are you beating yourself with a 'big stick'

Low Self Esteem can be cured! Low self esteem can be beaten:

Stop beating yourself up, low self esteem feeds on negative

messages and thoughts. <u>Silence your inner judge!</u> Stop trying to please other people, it is considerate when you care about others feelings, but your needs are just as important.

<u>Don't neglect yourself!</u>

Stop trying to be like someone else, this leads to a lack of self worth and confidence. You are unique and cannot be someone else.

Stop taking life or yourself so seriously. If you fail at something remember that every body fails on their way to succeeding, don't look on it as failure but as a means to learning, and last but not least stop wearing those non-authentic masks. They set you up for emotional pain and use up too much psychological energy.

"ANYONE WHO HAS NEVER MADE A MISTAKE HAS NEVER TRIED ANYTHING NEW" BY ALBERT EINSTEIN

Our self esteem can be as fragile as a butterfly's wings. We can be feeling strong and happy one minute, then someone can come along and crush us when we least expect it.

Why do people do this you may ask? Why are people so cruel?

The truth is it is often out of awareness, but sometimes it may be because the person is jealous, they may have a low self esteem of their own, they are hurting, they are angry with the world, they may have transference issues towards you (see next chapter), they may not have an understanding of what makes you crumble because of the masks that you wear, or your mask may make them feel weak, vulnerable or inadequate to name but a few.

There are people in this world who will try to blow your

candle out to make theirs shine brighter. **Stand bright on your own, and don't let other people have that much control over your self esteem?**

We can't be responsible for other people's feelings. We can respect, empathise and understand them but we can't and should not own them. We can hold their vulnerabilities, if they take off their masks, like the fragile butterfly that they are and ensure that we don't abuse their weaknesses, their sore spots.

If you know they fear rejection or exclusion then we can be mindful of this and try not to reject or exclude them.

We can ensure that if they have upset us we discuss this and not punish them with their own crumple buttons and reject or exclude them. We cannot take advantage of people's needs to be perfect or people pleasing and let them know that we accept them when they are imperfect and not trying to please. We can allow those that need to act tough all the time that we love their ability to be vulnerable.

We can empower them for being their true selves.

To protect our own self esteem we can recognise which people we don't feel good around and distance ourself from those people. They need to find their own way.

Keep away from people who try to belittle your ambitions. Small people always do that, but the really great make you feel that you, too can become great!
Mark Twain

Try to stay away from people who belittle you as a person. Surround yourself with people who accept you for who you are!

I had a friend who I thought was my friend until I realised

that every time I spent time with her I did not feel good about myself, she would criticise me, even say things that were not true about me just to make herself feel better, or look better in front of other people.

These type of people can be sometimes known as 'frienemies', they are not true friends. They often have a very low self esteem themselves. True friends would want you to feel good about yourself and would compliment you and affirm your achievements. Needless to say I ended that friendship. I decided that I only wanted people in my life that made me feel good about myself. Not the ones who only seemed to want to put me down. My world is a better place to be in.

Do you have any friends like this?

- Write down a list of your friends

- Tick the ones you feel good being around and note the ones that leave you feeling 'down about yourself'

- Tick the friends and tick the freinimies

- Do you really need the frenimies in your life?

- If so why?

Spend more time with the friends that make you feel good about yourself.

I would now like to share with you one of my favourite tools that I use with people with a low self esteem.   It also keeps my self esteem high.

Take a piece of A4 paper and put a line down the **middle.**

On the left hand side of the paper I would like you to write down the name of five significant people in your life that you really admire. (It does not matter if they are still with us or not).

This may take some time.

5 People that I admire:	
Anne	
Emma	
Claire	
Paul	
Karen	

Now write down on the right hand side all the things that you admire about them. Try to choose three different qualities for each person. In other words you cannot use the same quality more than once.

Remember that everyone has good qualities and not so good qualities, we are looking at their good qualities here. Do not turn to the next page until you have done this.

5 People that I admire:	What you admire about them
Anne	Caring, straightforward, brave
Emma	Funny, empathic, assertive
Claire	Kind, helpful, chatty
Paul	Loyal, spirited, loving
Karen	Honest, carefree, understanding

Tear the paper in half and put the left part in the bin, (the people you admire).

Write at the top of the page "I AM........." Now read out aloud all the things that you are.

"It is not possible to recognize these qualities in others unless you have them yourself!!!"

So yes all those qualities that you have written down, is you , as it's not possible to recognise qualities in others unless you have them yourself.

How neat is that?

Now what I would like you to do before you go any further. I would like you to turn that piece of paper about yourself into a poster, and I would also like you to make some little cards with your qualities on.

Now copy those posters around the house and keep your card in your bag or pocket and when you are having a low day. Go read your qualities.

Here's my example:

> **I AM.............**
>
> **Caring**
> **Straight forward**
> **Brave**
> **Funny**
> **Empathic**
> **Assertive**
> **Kind**
> **Helpful**
> **Chatty**
> **Loyal**
> **Spirited**
> **Loving**
> **Honest**
> **Carefree**
> **Understanding**

If I had asked you to write down **15** positives about yourself, would you have been able to do that? People with a low self esteem would struggle to name three.

Read your qualities out loud at least once a day, and particularly when your esteem is low. Remind yourself. Be compassionate to yourself.

Often we can be extremely compassionate towards others and yet extremely harsh towards ourselves. I often find myself asking clients "If this was a friend would you be this harsh on them" and they very rarely would, so why themselves?

Try using some compassion to change your mind, about your negative thoughts and feelings about yourself. Ask yourself the following questions:

1. What are the advantages of this self criticism?
2. What are the disadvantages of this self criticism?
3. Where will this self criticism eventually lead you?
4. What sort of person will it turn you into?
5. What is your greatest fear in giving up this self criticism?
6. What might others gain from you staying self critical?

Now lets look at the origins of this self attacking style and why people continue and submit or agree to it and why (e.g. habit, or fear based)?

1. When did you start to become self critical?
2. What was happening in your life?
3. Whose voice started the process?
4. What would have been your greatest fear in standing up to that critical other or voice in your head?
5. What would it take now to stop agreeing with it?
6. What are the credentials of this critic (external or internal)?
7. Does your inner critic have your best loving interests at heart?

Now have a go at writing yourself a compassionate letter.

The purpose of this exercise is to enable you to develop a new type of relationship with yourself and to get in touch with your more compassionate 'self':

1. Find some quiet time and a quiet place for yourself. (About an hour)
2. Read this carefully.
3. Relax and take a few slow breaths.
4. Bring to your mind a compassionate image, which may be an animal or a person that you perceive to be very nurturing.
5. Imagine this image talking to you, and this is what you write down.

The content of the letter should show clear empathy for your own distress e.g.

"It is understandable that you feel like .... because...."

Remember:

This is an experiment and not about doing things, right or wrong. It may take some practice to get the hang of it. Avoid using words such as 'should' or 'oughts'. Avoid any advice, be supportive and encouraging. Avoid "why don't you......" or "It will help you if....." Be helpful and caring of yourself.

To start the letter:

1. Try to feel that part of you that can be kind and understanding of others.
2. Be how you are when caring for someone you like.
3. Think about that part of you as the type of self you would like to be.
4. Think about the qualities you would like your compassionate self to have.

As you write the letter:

1. Now try to focus on the feelings of warmth and a genuine wish to help in the letter as you write it. Spend time breathing gently and really try as best as you can to let feelings of warmth be there for you.
2. Try to allow yourself to have *understanding* and *acceptance* for your distress.
3. Include times in your life when you have coped with difficulties before.
4. Include in your letter your efforts and the things you are able to do, your qualities and your strong points.
5. Understand that it does not help you to deal with the disappointment, loss or fear. So we need to be understanding and compassionate about the disappointment, loss and fear.
6. If you are having powerful feelings, then compassionately recognise these. Accept that negative emotions are part of being human and can become more powerful when we are distressed or depressed.
7. Accept that these emotions do not make us a bad person –

just a human being trying to cope with difficult feelings.

Ending the letter:

1. Think about what might be the compassionate thing to do when experiencing the above, at this moment or in the future.
2. Plan in your letter how you are going to bring compassion into action in your life.
3. If there are things you are avoiding or finding difficult to do,   write down some small steps to move you forward.
4. Try to write down steps and ideas that encourage you to do the things that you might find difficult.

Example letter:

Dear Linda,

I can see you are hurting right now and it is understandable that this feels painful for you as it links to similar experiences in your past.   But look how well you have coped with these experiences before and come through them in a positive way. It is these times in your life when you have recognised that you need to take care of yourself more, with extra bubble baths, relaxation and meditation. The qualities you have for taking care of others gives you the skills to take care of you.

It is human to think so negatively about yourself when you feel rejected, but you are a nice person and many people love you and care for you. Look at all the good things in your life and how clever of you to write this book and share with others your knowledge and skills.

The times that you have gone through difficulties in your

life have helped you in your role as a therapist; they have helped you to develop empathy and understanding for others. This time will be the same. You are very brave to stay with this pain and not run away like you usually do, it won't last forever and this is part of the healing process. It will stop those masks from developing and creating more pain in the future.

Remember to rub your tummy and say "I will take care of you, I will protect you."

Accept that you are a good person with many qualities, read your quality list again to remind you of this and know that your heart is and always will be in the right place.

Ask yourself if you were writing to someone else would you feel your letter is kind and helpful? Could you change anything to make it more warm and helpful?

Once you are able to accept yourself you can then begin to accept others in a more unconditional way.

Think of all the people or types of people that you dislike i.e. drug users, drinkers, loud, shy, opinionated people, obnoxious people, lazy people, workaholics, bullies etc., etc. These are all **'behaviours'** of people. They are not the '**WHOLE'** person.

Is it the behaviours that you dislike or the people? It is okay to say that I do not like this person's behaviour. Can you look beyond the behaviour and see the person's other more accepting qualities?

Try and see that the 'behaviour' is not the whole of this person. Everyone has good qualities as well as bad qualities, and remember that sometimes people's behaviours are the masks they use to protect their vulnerabilities and pain. Just like you do.

If you can accept others and their mistakes then you will be more able to accept your own. Only a small percentage of people reach a level of autonomy, where they can totally be accepting of 'self' and 'others'. However we feel much more psychologically healthy if we can make a start.

Back to 'you' - go to the bathroom and look yourself in the eye. Look yourself straight in the eye and see the real you. See the 'you' that messes up. See the 'you' that screams at the kids, shouts at your partner, burns the dinner etc. See the 'you' that is definitely not perfect.

Part of growing up is admitting to who you are, and accepting it, and not being so hard on yourself

Consider everything about yourself that drives you crazy! AND LOVE YOURSELF!! It will be a freeing experience for you. And you will be on your way to accepting yourself and others. Last but not least happiness leads to a good self esteem. If you are happy with yourself, your image, your personality, your behaviour, your career and your relationships then your self esteem will be high. **BE HAPPY!**

Unconconditionally me

I am who I am, you cannot change me so please do not try.
So let up with the criticisms, put downs and attempts to make me fit your "box" for me.
Face it, it is easier for you just to accept me as I am than to work at making me who you want me to be.

Of course you do not have to agree with what I say or do, just accept me as the human I am.

I shall wear purple

I am weak, have sinned, failed, and have made mistakes in my life. Hey that's what makes me the "unique me" that I am.

I will never be perfect, ideal or the "image" you want for me. Accept me for who I am as I accept you for who you are.

Let's have fun together and allow our "real selves" the freedom to be "us" – We can be a team of unconditional mutual love and acceptance if you relax and let it happen.
by Jim Messin

PERSONAL NOTES AND EXERCISES:

Chapter Six

"Transference"

THE PARTY

The smell, the taste, the sound, the touch will influence you to decide
On your friends, lovers or acquaintances and from those you wish to hide.
I scan the party of strangers the music's very loud
I hope to make some friendships from the faces in the crowd.
But that guy dances like the school bully, from twenty five years gone past,
I'll give him funny looks all night. Yeh! That should be a blast.
She looks like my English teacher she was always so nice to me
I wonder if she'd like this dance, I wonder if she's free.
He sounds like my bloody father, I better make sure I'm good,
Stand tall, be polite and courteous behave like he said I should
She feels like my ex girlfriend prickly, cold and hard
She offers me a cocktail and puts me on my guard.
Oh God here comes Rambo who walks just like my brother?
And the stunning girl I'm chatting up smells faintly like my mother.
I may as well go home now this parties quite a bore
When everyone I see here reminds me of before.

So many people I run from
Who remind me of my past?
Will I ever have a relationship?
That's guaranteed to last!
- Linda Mather 2010

This chapter you may find to be very deep, the complexity of 'transference' can have you feeling like you are on a roller coaster ride and need to get off don't get off enjoy the experience, enjoy the ride.

If you do get off and skip this chapter, I know that one day you will come back to it, as it is such an interesting topic. It is a topic that will help you to develop a deeper understanding of yourself and a non judgmental acceptance for others.

As well as needing to be fully accepting of yourself to enable you to dispose of your unhelpful masks, it is just as important to develop a deeper acceptance of others, and to do this you need to gain a heightened understanding of yourself and others and the way that as human beings we function.

If you do not like certain people or lack trust in them, your masks will just become thicker and multiply. Therefore, the more accepting that you are of other people, then the fewer masks you will need to wear.

Exploring your transference helps you to discover why you don't like a particular person and enables you to become more accepting of that person. It helps us to recognize the difficulties we sometimes have in developing relationships with some people in our lives, and more importantly the reasons why some people may not be able to relate to us. Learning why some people have difficulty relating to us can also help us to eliminate feelings of rejection.

Sigmund Freud known to be the 'Father' of psychotherapy introduced us to the fascinating idea of 'transference,' and learning about 'transference' will enable you to develop a deeper understanding of how relationships from the past can affect the way we relate to people in the present. It will help you to understand why some people do not like us and why we take a dislike to others for no apparent reason.

Once you understand this process you will be able to meet people 'freely' and attract healthier relationships.

To meet everything and everyone through stillness instead of mental noise
Is the greatest gift you can offer to the universe.
Eckhart Tolle

Transference means "to bring past experiences into the present.' Eric Berne simplified this by using the term 'rubber-banding back into a past experience.' Or 'putting a face on someone'. It is a psychological phenomenon in which we direct emotions and feelings often unconsciously from one person to another. This process is something that therapist monitor in the therapeutic relationship when a person receiving treatment applies feelings or expectations of another person on to the therapist and then begins to relate and interact with the therapist as if s/he were the other individual.

This can give a therapist an insight into how the client relates to significant others in their lives and patterns in their way of relating. The transference is often representative of a relationship from childhood.

Transference is a common occurrence among humans in various situations and may form the basis for certain relationship patterns in everyday life.

For example a work colleague that easily annoys you can unconsciously remind you of your often irritating younger sibling and so you relate to the colleague in the same was as you did them. Or you may have a co worker who is older and female that you treat with tenderness because she reminds you of your deceased mother. Equally if you had a poor experience with your mother you may treat her badly. Or maybe you mistrust a romantic partner simply because a previous partner cheated on you. This is all transference whereby you are projecting feelings and emotions on to a person from your past.

Transference may be positive or negative. Positive transference can lead you to view the other as kind or vulnerable, this can lead you to rescue the person, which you did or didn't do to a significant other in your past. Negative transference might cause you to direct anger or painful feelings towards the other which belonged to the significant other in your past.

When this happens in a therapeutic relationship the therapist may be able to use these emotions to help the client achieve greater understanding.

For the most part of this chapter, we will be looking at 'negative transference,' later we will take a look at 'positive transference.'

A simple explanation of 'negative transference,' for those of you who have had children, you may recall spending quite some time thinking about names for the new arrival. Someone may suggest a name of someone you knew from the past. This person may have behaved badly, dressed scruffily, smelt, and had a permanent runny nose or some other characteristic that you did not like.

You then discount that name with *"oh no I don't want my child called that"*

A reality check would tell you that this does not mean your baby will be anything like the person in your past; however we rarely do a reality check and often just dismiss the name completely.

This is also sometimes what we do to people, discount them because consciously or unconsciously they remind us of someone we disliked, or treated us badly from our past. This could be 'in' or 'out' of our conscious awareness.

On a conscious level we may say things like *"He's a Gemini, the last Gemini I knew................."* This could stop you from forming a relationship with a Gemini. Logic tells us that not all Gemini's are the same, and the other Gemini's behaviour is more likely to be down to his/her own experiences, than their birth sign.

There are lots of characteristics/behaviours that can trigger conscious transference i.e.

- o Eyebrows that meet in the middle
- o Someone who drinks heavily
- o Someone who sulks
- o Clothes/style
- o Perfume

Transference that is on a conscious level we can reality test, we can change our thoughts too *"well actually he did not behave in that way just because his eyebrows met in the middle,"* or other people may reality test our beliefs for us.

However, on an unconscious level, we may take an instant dislike to someone, without knowing why. This may prevent us from developing a relationship with them. We find ourselves saying something like *"I don't know why I don't like her, there's just something about her"*

We may not even recognize what we are doing, just notice feeling uncomfortable around someone, or struggling to relate to a person, or become irritated with a person for no reason at all. We may start to avoid that person due to those feelings and never know why.

These triggers are a lot more subtle, i.e.

- o The way someone stands/walks
- o The colour/shape of their eyes
- o Their colour, shape or gender
- o The way they speak/mannerisms

Remember that this is often all out of our own awareness. An example of my own transference, when I was doing my therapy training, I was really struggling to relate to an afro Caribbean lady on my course. I avoided working with her for skills practice. I never really had a conversation with her and if I did my guard was up, out of awareness; my 'tough cookie' mask came on.

During the course we were asked to think about someone on the course that we were struggling to relate to. The point of the exercise was to try and recognize any transference issues we may have towards another group member.

I used the skills that I will be sharing with you and asked myself a set of questions. Through this I was able to recognize that I was rubber banding back into a past experience.

When I was delivering my first child I had an afro Caribbean midwife. My first labour as many first deliveries are was 20 hours long. I was scared, vulnerable and naïve. The midwife was unsupportive and showed very little empathy. She was controlling, rough and critical, making the experience of childbirth an unnecessarily unpleasant one.

Further exploration I recognized that fifteen years later when I had an hysterectomy and was in hospital a afro Caribbean lady roughly placed me on a commode which left me in pain. So on two occasions I had been vulnerable and reliant on someone's care and kindness I didn't receive it. It just so happens that they were with someone of this culture (I have since met some lovely and kind Caribbean people). So on an unconscious level I did not feel safe sharing my vulnerabilities with this lady due to experiences from the past. I was putting the head of these two ladies on the shoulders of my colleague.

Skills practice and the emotional journey experienced by therapists in training can open up one's vulnerabilities and encourages us to be our true selves to a certain extent. I needed to keep myself safe with this lady. I unconsciously did not trust this lady with my 'weak' self, my real self just in case she abused me or treated me roughly, and this was why I avoided her.

However, once I was able to understand and work through this transference it enabled me to meet this lady 'freely.' I was then able to build a relationship with her. Ironically we became good friends. She turned out to be a lovely lady, and nothing like 'the midwife or nurse' from my past.

If you judge people, you have no time to love them.
Mother Theresa

I had unconsciously judged her due to my own transference. Rubber banding back into a past experience and putting 'the midwifes' face/personality onto my colleague. Just think, if I had not worked through this, I may never have had the opportunity of really getting to know this lovely lady.

Exploring your own transference

To enable you to think about your own transference is there someone in your life that you have avoided, taken an instant dislike to or someone that you are currently in conflict with. Is it your transference? Ask yourself the following questions:

- Who do they remind you of from your past?

This may take some time because you are delving deep into your unconscious, if you can't think of anyone carry on reading but come back to those thoughts when you are pottering along in your daily routine.

If however you recognise a dislike of this person because they remind you of someone from your past. This is your transference. Ask yourself:

- What is it about them that remind you of this person?

- Is this evidence enough for you to dislike this person?

This will enable you to work through your transference and separate the past from the present. Maybe there is more than one person. This may help you to further develop your relationships with these people.

Treat people as you do your pictures
And place them in their best light.
Jennie Jerome Churchill

How many people have passed through our lives due to our transference? How many relationships with people have we missed out on? Negative transference can block us from forming healthy relationships with others.

If when doing these exercises you found that the person you disliked, avoided or had conflict with did not remind you of anyone from your past, it may not be transference.

Try asking yourself this questions:

- Is my attitude towards this person inherited from my parents?

Sometimes we inherit our parent's beliefs about a type of person. For example if your parents gave you messages like 'never trust a man who's eyebrows meet in the middle,' then it's possible that we have inherited the same belief.

- Reality test that belief/contamination.

As adults we do not have to hold on to the beliefs of others. After all think about some of the messages our parents gave us when we were little that we don't hold on to:

- Eat all your vegetables or you won't have curly hair
- Don't sit on a cold step or you will get piles
- Eat your greens or you will lose your eye sight, you don't see rabbits going into an optician
- Put your tooth under the pillow or the tooth fairy won't come

Do we cling on desperately to those beliefs when we reach adulthood? No we reality test them and discard them. Therefore we can do that with any beliefs that were inherited.

Again if the above is not the case, try this:

- Is this person similar to me?

Sometimes others may display characteristics or behaviours similar to our own. These may be the parts of us that we don't like, the parts of us that we try to hide. The parts we hide behind our own masks.

For example, we may hide the 'weak' side of our self. Therefore we may not like other people who appear weak. Or if part of our personality may be to be opinionated it is highly unlikely that we will relate to another opinionated person.

To explore this ask yourself:

- What do I see in this person that I don't like about myself?

Or it may just be that you don't like this person's behaviour, and it is not transference at all. However the exploration will enable you to see if you are meeting this person 'freely,' developing healthier relationships along the way.

Also be mindful that what you don't like about the person is a mask they wear to protect themselves, so by allowing them to be themselves, you might like what is underneath this mask.

It is extremely important to be able to explore your transference when you are working within the caring profession or working with people in general. That way all the people that you work with will get the same treatment. You will be offering them an empathic, non judgmental and congruent service.

If you are really brave further exploration could be to ask yourself:

- Am I jealous of this person?
- If so why?
- Do I need to be?
- Where's the evidence of the above

In your personal growth it is very important to own your own feelings, and explore them to prevent you from making a hash out of interpersonal relationships, which we can all do at times.

Transference can impact on our feelings too. Certain situations can make us feel 'bad' and this is because we are re-experiencing similar situations from the past that made us feel 'bad'.

Have you ever been called to your boss's office and all the

way there you have anxiety - wondering what you have done wrong. When you get there it is something positive, like you have a pay rise! You may be rubber-banding back to your school days when you got called to the headmaster's office and got a telling off.

Often when we go for an interview for a job we will experience feelings of transference. We may be rubber-banding back to all the jobs we did not get in the past creating anxiety, butterflies, lethargy, all symptoms that could initiate a 'bad' interview.

The idea is to disconnect the rubber band, and bring yourself back into the 'here and now'.

A technique I use in a situation like this is to wear a rubber band on my wrist,. (Anxiety is a fear, it is something that has previously happened and we then believe it will happen in the future), when the anxiety starts I flick the elastic band. This causes slight physical pain in the here and now. I am therefore bringing myself back to the 'here and now' and not reliving a past experience and projecting it on to my future. I may have to do this a couple of times, but it works.

Try it, but be careful you don't flick it too hard. By the time you go into the threatening situation you will be much more calm and relaxed and be able to manage this in a healthier way.

Now for you:

Think about a recent situation in which you were under stress and which ended unpleasantly or unsuccessfully for you.

- Think what bad 'feeling' you experienced during that situation.

- Bring back the memory of a similar unpleasant situation with the same bad 'feeling' from your childhood or past.

- What age were you?

- Who was there?

- What was happening?

Once you are aware of what past situation you were replaying, this will remind you that people in the 'here and now' are in fact different from the people in your past; you can then begin disconnecting the rubber band. Techniques to help you to do this are:

- **Self-talk** - this is a new experience, this is today not yesterday. I know more about things now than I did then. I am good at what I do. This is not then this is NOW!

- **Rubber band**s – as described earlier, wear a rubber band around your wrist and prang it when you feel anxious. It will bring you back to the 'here and now' and relieve the anxiety. You may have to keep doing this.

- **Tapping** - Use two fingers to tap another part of your body, your hand, your wrist, the side of your eyes, this again will bring you back to the 'here and now'

- **Scanning** - scan the room for a picture on the wall or in a magazine and focus on the colours in the picture again bringing you back into the 'Here and now'.

- **Reframing** - If it is a job interview for example, imagine that you are going into the room to 'teach', you are going to tell these people who you are and what skills you have, nothing more, nothing less. If a job comes at the end of it then hey ho that's a bonus.

There are times in our life when we come across people who dislike us. As most of us have a need to be liked, if not loved this can be quite painful.

There is more hunger for love and appreciation in this world than for bread.
- Mother Theresa

This can create an unpleasant feeling. It can be painful, and it can have an affect on our thinking, feeling and behaviour, and of course, can create new masks to wear, or bring to the surface old ones. We often internalise other people's dislike for us.

We can let it affect us sometimes profoundly, yet it could be down to their transference. It may have nothing to do with us personally.

To be completely free we have to forget what other people think of us, otherwise our world becomes a prison. We will spend too much time trying to be what we think others want us to be, trying to be liked, to be loved and even then we may not get what we want and all that time and energy has been wasted. Next time that you have a sense that someone does not like you try 'batting it back,' instead of internalising it.

Imagine their 'dislike' or 'comments' to be a tennis ball. Use an imaginary tennis racket to bat the ball back. This is their stuff not yours so try not to own it. This stops you from internalising their dislike and subsequently stops negative thinking about yourself, negative feelings and consequently negative behaviour.

Remember though that other people's transference could be on an unconscious level. They may not be aware that they are rubber banding back to past experiences. It's not always a good idea to bring them to awareness ~ not unless they are involved in their own personal growth, as it tends to trigger peoples defenses. They may become angry with you; people will not look at themselves until they are ready and become touchy if forced. This learning is to enable you to not take peoples dislike of you personally, and to see that it could be other people's transference. It is for your growth.

We cannot be responsible for other people's transference. We can empathise with their past experience if we know what it is. But, we have no control over it, no matter how much we try to be liked. We can only explore and work on our own transference issues. And remember, it might actually be your 'mask' they don't like!

It's interesting to think about how much transference there is in the world, that we are not always aware of, and the effect that this can have on people's lives.

Imagine you are a judge or a magistrate. Someone is stood in the dock on a burglary charge. S/he reminds you (consciously or unconsciously) of the person who bullied you at school, or a teacher you disliked. How many years would you sentence him to compared to someone you had no negative transference for.

I can recall my daughter, when she was at college going for an interview for a Saturday job at a small newsagent in the town. I used this shop often and knew that most of the assistants past and present were middle aged and blonde. My daughter is a brunette. She did not get the job.

I did wonder at the time if this was anything to do with the manager's transference, maybe he was rubber banding back into past experiences, linked to his early beliefs about middle aged blondes or young brunettes. It could, of course have been that my daughter flunked the interview, even though she felt that she had done quite well.

This was an experience which may have affected her self esteem and had an impact on her confidence at future interviews, developing a negative belief about herself. She may have experienced feelings of rejection or not being 'good enough'. It may have assisted her in developing another mask, to protect herself from future rejection. We will never know, but the explanation of the 'transference' process to my daughter stopped her from internalising the 'rejection.' So, that has to be positive!

I later found myself looking at other shop assistants, doctors/dentist receptionists, travel agents etc and interestingly enough there were similarities amongst the staff. Was this 'transference' or 'co-incidence?'

It certainly gave me food for thought. Have some fun and look around yourself!

As well as negative transference, we can also have what is known as positive transference. This is rubber banding back to positive experiences of people in our past. 'Liking' people because they remind you of someone you liked or whom were good to you in the past. Again, this can be on a conscious level or an unconscious level.

We may, or others may develop a dependency due to this transference. They could see us or we could see others as 'the good mummy' or 'the supportive big sister.' Be aware that this in itself can create unhealthy relationships.

In my early therapist days I was only slightly aware of 'positive transference' - I was working with a young girl who was 17 and around the same age as my son. My relationship with my son was poor at the time and he was forever telling me what a bad mum I was. This impacted on my 'be perfect mask' and was very painful. I internalised it as true. Of course in hindsight it wasn't I was setting boundaries that were not compatible with his lifestyle at the time. Love him dearly.

My supervisor picked up in my clinical supervision how I was letting this client push the boundaries in therapy; I was being the 'people pleasing/perfect therapist.' I did not want to be 'the bad mum.' This was positive transference that was unhelpful in the therapeutic relationship, and the client was not making any changes. Once I was brought to this awareness in supervision, I firmed up the boundaries and ironically the client began to make changes.

Feeling like you're on a roller coaster ride?

The idea is to meet people freely, without rubber banding back to the past and without letting your relationships of the past impact on relationships with others in the present.

If relationships are stuck, in conflict, or suffocating, then you now have another tool to explore the process, if you wish.

However, to now throw another spanner in the works!!!

Not all 'dislike' for others is transference, it is important to bear in mind that our memory can also be a tool to help us to avoid repeating past mistakes, and attracting relationships that are not so good for us. It may at times be our gut instinct so it is as I described earlier important to listen to our head and our hearts.

Process this learning for a while. Explore your own transference issues. As uncomfortable as it may feel, it does assist you on your journey of emotional growth. It helps you to be more accepting of others and improves your relationships now and in the future.

The great teachings unanimously emphasize that all the peace, wisdom, and joy in the world are already within us; we don't have to gain, develop or attain them.
We're like a child standing in a beautiful park with his eyes shut tight.
We don't need to imagine trees, flowers, deer, birds and sky; We merely need to open our eyes and realise what is already here,
who we really are.
Bo Lozoff

You are now off the roller coaster ride. Are you ready for the 'big dipper?!'

As well as transference Freud talked about 'counter-transference.' This is <u>'our response to someone else's transference.'</u>

Imagine that you reminded someone of a bully from their schooldays, who had made their lives a misery. They may approach you quite defensively. What would your response be?

If you too became defensive or angry, you could be responding to this person's transference, with counter transference possibly from experiences in your own past.

Or imagine someone who saw you as 'the good mummy' and you respond by mothering him this could be your counter transference, a little like my response to my 17 year old client, my need to be the 'good mummy' was my counter transference.

To do this may have triggered the start of a victim/rescuer relationship, the type of relationship that I experience to be a very unhealthy one. Worse still it may trigger you to accept all types of abuse from the person you are mothering.

For example you are in a relationship with someone who was abandoned at birth by their mother, you have great empathy for him. However, each time you go out with your friends he is miserable, on your return he is horrible to you, calling you all sorts of abusive names. Unbeknown to him he has rubber banded back to that earlier experience of being abandoned and his transference towards you is that you are the mother that abandoned him.

You are aware of this, but it is not in his conscious awareness so you mother him, ignoring the abuse. This is your counter transference of trying to be the 'good mother.' This pattern of relating will continue until he can reach an awareness of his unconscious processes. He is getting his maternal needs met and you are feeling rubbish due to the abuse.

You would continue with this way of relating until you developed 'empathy boundaries' and did not respond to his behaviour with your counter transference.

Counter transference is when we transfer our feelings in response to another person's transference, which stems from relationships in our past (either our most recent past or from years ago).

Look at the following behaviours and write down your immediate responses:

1. Someone who is hostile towards you.
2. Someone who believes you are a semi divine being
3. Someone who gets angry with you
4. Someone who is going one up (one upmanship)
5. Someone who sits dejectedly in the corner

It's possible that, if you have been honest, your responses are your counter transference. Look at the following examples, were your responses similar?

Someone who is hostile towards you	DEFENSIVE
Someone who believes you are a semi divine being	ARROGANT
Someone who gets angry with you	ANGRY
Someone who is going one up (One upmanship)	RUDE
Someone who sits dejectedly in the corner	RESCUING

If you respond with your counter transference you are more likely to be in conflict or difficulties within your relationships. We cannot control other people's transference, but we can be responsible for our own responses once we are aware.

The idea is to respond from the 'here and now,' freely, and not respond from our own past issues, or from our masks. It's important also to be honest. Here are some examples of healthy, here and now responses:

Healthy response

Hostile	*I sense your hostility and I am wondering what is going on for you*
Semi Divine Being	*I am worried that you see me as something I am not*
Anger	*I can see you are angry with me can we sit down and talk*
Going one up	*It is great when we can be more equal in our way of relating*
Sits dejectedly	*I can see you are in pain, help me to understand*

The more conflict we have in relationships, the stronger our old masks become, and new ones are born. The most noticeable way in which transference can affect our lives, is when we rubber back into past experiences in situations such as being called in to see the boss, a trip to the doctors or communicating with people that we see as more powerful than ourselves.

We may as previously discussed rubber band back into our childhood experiences of being back at school. We can start to feel anxious, be stuck for words. All the feelings that you felt then can appear in the 'now'.

In situations like this use the techniques previously mentioned and ground yourself by reminding yourself that this is NOW and then was then. The technique I find most helpful is the rubber band on my wrist and then to prang myself when the anxiety starts; this is a good tool for bringing you back to the present, as it is instant.

In a nutshell the Psychological definition of transference is the experience of feelings to a person, which do not befit that person and which actually apply to another. Essentially, a person in the present is reacted to as though he were a person in the past.

Finally, we can also experience rubber banding back into pleasant or unpleasant events by other senses such as touch, smell, hearing and taste.

Have you ever been somewhere and had an overwhelming sense of happiness, joy, fear or anxiety, and don't know why? Chances are you are rubber banding back to the past from the tuning in of your other senses.

For example I always feel good when I pass the bakery counter at the local supermarket. The smell of freshly baked bread reminds me of the happy times I spent with my grandmother who often baked her own bread.

Likewise I get knots in my stomach when I smell a certain kind of disinfectant. I was able to link this back to childhood experiences of being in hospital.

Sometimes we have these 'experiences' and ignore the feelings, or describe them as deja vu - I've been here before. Maybe you have, or maybe the smell, taste, sound or sight is tied to a past experience, one that maybe you struggle to remember.

Be still and cease your endless chatter; Think upon the things that matter.

Never mind about the past, time is passing much too fast for
you to sit and ponder on thoughts and actions long since gone.
Source unknown

PERSONAL NOTES & EXERCISES:

Chapter Seven

"Psychological wounds"

CLEANING OUT OLD WOUNDS

**"Some people are afraid of what they might find if they try to analyse themselves too much,
but you have to crawl into your wounds to discover where your fears are.
Once the bleeding starts, the cleansing can begin."
-Tori Amos**

Have you ever picked the scar from a wound before it has healed? Or have you heard the saying "Pouring salt on an old wound?" Imagine how painful this would be. This is what we experience when someone picks at or pours salt on an old psychological or emotional wound that has never been healed.

Once you have been wounded, or perceived to have been wounded then to re-experience a similar incident is like putting salt on an already existing wound. That is because when we develop a wound we become sensitive to factors that would not usually bother us.

This is why different things affect different people in different ways. We all have different wounds, depending on our own personal experiences. This is also why it is sometimes difficult to understand why some people are upset over things that others would not generally get upset about; chances are that it is because it has penetrated an already open wound.

Why do some people feel bad when someone promises to call and does not and yet for others it is no real issue?

Why do you think some people hate the feeling of being out of control, and yet others are far more laid back? Why do some people deal with rejection much better than others? Why are some people more able to confront abuse than others?

It is because rejection, abandonment, being out of control, abuse is some peoples wound and not that of others. This is what makes us 'all the same' in a sense but also different. We all carry invisible wounds from our past.

If we suffer painfully when experiencing for example rejection or abandonment it could be because people who did not approve of us rejected us in the past, and so whenever someone ignores us in the present it hurts like hell. Not because it should hurt, but because it touched an old wound and reminded us of a past hurt. Again this can all be out of our conscious awareness.

Applying for a job and getting a rejection letter for example, would upset most people, but people with a fear of 'rejection' would be devastated and feel broken. It is because we all have different 'crumple buttons,' different wounds.

I always say to people if it has affected you profoundly, to a point where it limits your ability to function and/or manifests into depression then it is likely that it has re-opened and early wound, an early experience that was at the time painful for you.

If you try to just escape or forget about these wounds, they don't go away, they will come back to remind you that they are there each time you feel rejected or hurt or abused or even engulfed or indeed out of control.

These wounds make you vulnerable! Things that do not

bother some people can prevent others from sleeping at night, because they are wounds that haven't healed.

Has there been a time in your life where you have been frozen by your emotional pain.

Have you been unable to function and yet not understood why this has affected you so much? Chances are that whatever you have experienced to bring on this pain has hooked into an early wound.

Take some time to explore this.

- What happened to you?
- Has this happened before?
- Is this a pattern, do you always fold when this happens to you?

Before we can heal any of these wounds we should first identify what they are, where they came from and know the reason behind the wound. When you know the root cause, healing the wound is the easy part.

If you block out these wounds or ignore them, they never leave you alone; you will continue to revisit the pain time after time, each time you feel the negative feeling that is your early wound. This will impact on the development of masks that you wear, to protect you from ever feeling this pain again. Unfortunately they do not work; they only serve to create more pain.

Psychodynamic therapy which is often more long term

therapy helps you to heal those wounds and part of the process is to revisit those early experiences and re experience the pain. A good therapist will hold that pain and nurture that pain to heal an experience whereby you possibly did not get this nurturing and holding process. This is usually done well into the therapy to enable the relationship to develop between you and your therapist and to enable you both to see what these wounds are by talking and exploration.

It can be a painful process but from my own personal experience, once you have done this, when a familiar situation arises again in your life, although it can be hurtful, it is nothing like the overwhelming emotion that you once felt and much easier to deal with. It is not until then that you realise that the healing has occurred, your wound has been healed.

There will be no need to develop another mask, another defense to protect yourself. You will find yourself dealing with the situation in a very different way.

A life lived in fear is a life not fully lived

Once you have identified your wounds, and have recognized their origin, then the healing can begin.

Identifying your pain is about allowing yourself to 'feel it,' staying with the pain. Often when we feel an uncomfortable, negative feeling we do our utmost to avoid it, we run from it like it is a tsunami.

We do this by keeping busy, using substances such as drugs or alcohol, gambling, going for a walk, going to the gym, reading a book, sexual activity etc. A suppression of what we are feeling.

Although these are coping strategies that may work for you,

they are quick fixes. The pain does not go away, it will return when you least expect it and bite you on the bum. It will be a double whammy, because you have not yet healed the original wound. It will return when someone pours salt on that deep and open wound.

What is the worst that can happen to you if you stay with the pain? You won't die. It won't send you mad. It will be extremely uncomfortable and you may cry for England. But crying is healthy; it is a release of all the emotion to allow you to then think more clearly.

Ignoring the pain will only assist you in developing more masks.

Ask yourself:

- What is the thing that upsets you the most?
- What do you fear the most?
- What causes you pain that renders you dysfunctional?

Emotional growth is a life long journey, just as you work through one part of 'self,' something else may come along and the work begins again, but each time you do this you will feel better and function in a more healthy way. The first time is the hardest because you don't know what to expect, after this you will find it easier to work on all your emotional wounds as they arise.

The whole of life is a journey, and as soon as you know the answers, you get completely lost again

Being lost is part of life's process, staying lost will cause you more emotional turmoil.

Find a safe place at a safe time.

- Sit or lay comfortably.
- Put your hand on your stomach or wherever you feel the emotional pain and ask yourself:
- What am I feeling right now?
- When have I felt like this before?
- How many times do I feel like this?
- What is the theme running through these experiences?

This will help you to discover your wound and help you to take the first step towards healing.

Imagine someone cut you with a knife on your arm and before this had chance to heal, someone else cut you in the same place. Can you imagine how much this would hurt? Then someone cut you again and again in this same place. What would you imagine you would do?

My guess is that you would develop strategies to protect yourself from being cut in that same place again. Maybe you would buy a thick jacket or wear a plaster cast. Or you might avoid going out of the house or shout at people to keep them at a distance.

That is how you may react to a physical wound. We do exactly the same thing with psychological or emotional wounds, although these wounds are usually invisible and much harder to describe, and are not always in our conscious awareness.

When we have experienced something painful and we re-experience that same pain, whether that is physical or emotional, we develop strategies, behaviours and masks to protect ourselves. To stop being hurt in the same place again.

However, I will endeavor to show you in this chapter how those strategies and masks actually set you up for further pain and do **not** in fact protect you.

Turn your wounds into wisdom

Exploring your psychological wound can be painful. Again I would recommend that if your early life experiences were particularly traumatic that you do this work in a safe environment with a reputable therapist.

To give you a better understanding of psychological wounds we will explore five primary wounds.

These are:

Abuse,
Abandonment
Rejection
Engulfment
Neglect

There are needless to say, various degrees of these wounds and also different situations that may come under these headings. For example:

Abandonment

There are mild to severe forms of abandonment.

➤ Mild would perhaps be someone who got lost when out shopping with mum. For two minutes that felt like two hours they may have felt abandoned.

➤ Moderate may be someone who was left with a child minder for two days without any explanation of where their parent had gone or when they were coming back may experience feelings of abandonment.

➤ Severe may be someone who has been fostered or adopted and experiences feelings of abandonment, or someone whose parents left them at home and never returned.

Don't forget it is how we internalize and experience these events, not everyone who has been adopted will experience feelings of abandonment and someone who got lost shopping with mum may experience overwhelming feelings of abandonment.

The same applies to all of the named wounds. The silent treatment when a child can leave you fearing rejected. Likewise one parent leaving or dying can leave you with the wound of rejection.Being swore at, name calling or no emotional attachment, being hit or worse can leave you with the wound of abuse. Not being cared for, not being educated sufficiently, or taken to medical appointments, right through to being left in a cot all day with no stimulation can be experienced as neglect. Having an over protective parent to someone who allows you no independence can create a fear of engulfment.

If your wound is severe in nature then I would strongly advise that you do this work which could be extremely painful with a therapist. It is also important to remember that our wounds could be perceived experiences, and they can be healed with the right help.

Let's look at a case study:

A child is put into childcare at a young age while both parents go to work, this child unbeknown to his/her parents feels hurt. This same child experiences the following events during her life:

1. Mum goes into hospital to have another baby
2. Mum and Dad separate – Dad sees very little of the children
3. At first school she is rejected by a group of friends
4. At second school her best friend moves away
5. Her first boyfriend 'dumps her'
6. She unfairly gets dismissed from her first job

S/he internalizes all this as 'rejection' and feels a stronger degree of pain after each incident. Almost like being cut several times in the same wound. **Oooch!**

Remember that a lot of kids manage this sort of situation quite well, and may internalise other situations to be difficult.

This is how each individual child may internalises different situations. They do not at a young age have the resources yet to reality test, to 'check things out.' As adults we have the ability to understand why and how, but as children we don't. To be the 'perfect' parent we would need to be able to mind read, constantly check out how our children are feeling, how certain situations have impacted on them. This would be impossible as we are 'human beings' too although I guess our teenage siblings would argue that point, and let's face it would they tell us if we asked?

THIS IS NOT A TOOL TO BEAT OURSELVES UP AS PARENTS. IT IS A TOOL TO HELP US TO UNDERSTAND OUR OWN PATHOLOGY.

This is not a tool to criticize our parents either. Most parents do their best whilst surviving life, and life experiences of their own. They will not always get things right and what affects one of their children will have absolutely no affect on the other. It is the way individual children internalize their experience.

What was your childhood like?

> Write down some of the things in your own childhood that had an impact on you.
> How did you feel?
> Does this experience impact on your resilience to this now?
> Does a similar experience affect you emotionally?

These are possibly your early wounds that have not as yet been healed. Be aware that you may have more than one wound and it may be about working on each one individually.

My guess is that this girl in this case study that clearly has a primary wound of rejection may begin to develop strategies, behaviours, thoughts and of course masks to protect her from further rejections, just as she would if this was physical pain.

Let's look at what those strategies/behaviours, thoughts and masks may be:

PSYCHOLOGICAL WOUND
REJECTION

↓

| PROTECTIVE BEHAVIOURS , THOUGHTS AND MASKS |

↓

BEHAVIOUR	*THOUGHTS*	*MASK*
People please	"If I please everyone they will not reject me"	GOOD GIRL
Be strong	"If I'm tough they won't hurt me"	TOUGH COOKIE
Push people away	"If I don't get close then I won't get kicked"	ICE QUEEN
Lash out	"If I hit them first, they can't hit me"	MISS ANGRY
Try hard	"If I'm perfect they won't get rid of me"	MISS PERFECT
Act the clown	"If I'm funny they will want me to stick around"	CO-CO THE CLOWN

Now look at each of these behaviours, thoughts and masks and ask the question

- ➤ "Does this protect her from further rejection?"
- ➤ "What is likely to happen to this girl when she behaves in
- ➤ this way and wears these masks?"

Let's look at if these behaviours will protect her from being rejected or are they more likely to set her up for further rejection?

BEHAVIOUR	THOUGHTS	MASK	PROTECT
People please	"If I please everyone they will not reject me"	GOOD GIRL	NO
Be strong	"If I'm tough they won't hurt me"	TOUGH COOKIE	NO
Push people away	"If I don't get close then I won't get kicked"	ICE QUEEN	NO
Lash out	"If I hit them first, they can't hit me"	MISS ANGRY	NO
Try hard	"If I'm perfect they won't get rid of me"	MISS PERFECT	NO
Act the clown	"If I'm funny they will want me to stick around"	CO-CO THE CLOWN	NO

They will set her up for further rejection! This in turn will help her to build up further resentments and stronger masks. Let's face it, who wants to be around:

"A tough, goodie two shoes, who fluctuates between being a clown, being perfect then lashing out in anger resulting in freezing you out?"

These are the masks this girl wears. How often would you suppose that she gets rejected? How exhausting to be all these people all of the while. How much psychological energy would you imagine this would take, depleting her of all her physical energy!

Underneath all this she is vulnerable, messes up occasionally and gets scared sometimes. What is wrong with that? She's a human being, why does she pretend not to be? She hides the 'real self' the part of her that is the same as the rest of us.

Could this be for fear she may be rejected, and does this stop her from being rejected or does it in fact set her up for further rejection?

(It is important to remember that even as children we all internalize things differently, some children will thrive from this experience – remember the two brothers and the bike incident from earlier in this book and how differently they internalized their experiences. As parents we can only do our best for our children, we can't possible know how our children might internalize the things we feel we're doing for the best).

Think about one of your own psychological wounds.

To help you to do this, think about things that have happened in your life that has caused you intense emotional pain.

Look for a pattern of events. Some other examples or primary wounds are:

Loss
Being out of control
Loneliness
Silent treatment
Conflict

Now draw the same diagram as above and write down all the things you do and think, and what masks you wear to protect yourself from re experiencing any of the above or your own wound. Then ask yourself the following questions:

- Do they actually protect you?
- If so, where's the evidence.
- Do they usually set you up for more of the same pain?
- If so, think of some experiences where this has happened.

So what do we do now, how can we change this pattern of behaviour, how can we remove these helpful masks? The answer is to change, to start removing these masks, one at a time and be your true self.

Can you see that these masks have not been altogether healthy for you? Do not knock these strategies, they have helped you to survive up to now, they may have stopped you from falling to pieces at times, but think about the times where they have caused you more harm than good.

Is now the time to look at healthier strategies. If so what we need to think about is developing new behaviours, we need to learn how to think differently and we need to let go of these well-worn masks!

Let's look at the earlier case study and what changes this girl could make:

NEW BEHAVIOURS

Old behaviours	New behaviours
People please	Learn to be more assertive and say "NO!"
Being strong	Show people her vulnerable side to be accepted
Push people away	Get close to people again, learn to trust
Lash out at people	Express anger in a healthier way
Try hard	Accept herself as imperfect, a human being
Act the clown	Be true self to be liked, still be funny but not as a mask to hide your true feelings.

Look at the old behaviours and the new ones. Which person would you like the most?

Now do a box like the one above and look at the masks you would like to discard and new behaviours.

Which sides of you do you like the best? If it is the new behaviours start putting them into practice. These are ways in which you can change and let go of old masks. Find some self help books around the behaviours you would like to change. For example if you feel you need to be less 'people pleasing' and more assertive, then buy yourself a assertiveness book, go on a assertiveness course, or find yourself a good therapist.

There is always a chance that you may still get hurt, but I can assure you the hurt will be less painful when you are being your 'true self' and this has got to be much better than being satisfied with lukewarm relationships, and hiding our vulnerabilities.

When you live life hiding behind your masks? When you enter phony relationships with phony masks you rob yourself of acceptance, intimacy, freedom, true friendship and true love.

People who reject you for being yourself are not happy with who they are and are not meant to be in your life. Enjoy your life with genuine like-minded people who accept you for who you really are.

All love that does not have true friendship for its base is like a mansion built upon the sand!

PERSONAL NOTES & EXERCISES:

Chapter Eight

"Change"

**Change yourself slowly
And cheerfully.
Conditions will change immediately
And unimaginably.**

~

**The mind thinks
That any change
Is painful.
The heart feels
That any change
Is powerful.**

- Sri Chinmoy

To change you need to challenge yourself. Take **'lle'** away from challenge and you get **'change.'**

As well as working on changing our behaviours we have developed to protect ourselves we need to also work on our way of thinking. It is often our attitude, thoughts and behaviour that create the events we are experiencing. Which in turn help us to develop the masks that we wear.

CBT or Cognitive behavioural therapy is growing in popularity these days. CBT theorists would say that most of the 'bad feelings' we have come from negative thoughts or distortions, and that through identifying the lie behind the thought we can change the way that we feel. The belief is that thinking, emotions and behaviours intertwine very closely and each can change the others.

So are you ready to start looking at the way that you think? And learn how your thoughts can trigger negative emotions, physical symptoms which then can affect the way that we behave, and of course the mask that we put on.

If the video goes wrong, we troubleshoot. If our business is failing, we troubleshoot. How many of us actually troubleshoot our own lives. It's because of this that the same horrible things happen to us time and time again.

We don't stop to ask why??? Let's troubleshoot now. Imagine you had the following belief:

"All wo/men are a waste of space, they always let you down. You're better off not getting too close to anyone and then you can't get hurt"

This belief could affect the way that you feel, the way that you behave socially and support you in developing a 'mask.' Maybe this line of thinking would create a 'Jack the lad,' 'tough cookie' or 'ice maiden' mask.

It could make you behave in abusive ways towards the gender you think is a 'waste of space'. It will assist you in attracting the wrong people for you, and subsequently set you up for further pain. And of course it is a LIE! Not all women or men are a waste of space.

Let's look at what this cycle of thought may create:

Thoughts
All wo/men are
a waste of space

Behaviour:
Isolate self
Drink heavily
Act tough
Lash out

CBT CYCLE

Feelings:
Lonliness
Anger
Frustration
Depression

Physical symptoms:
Butterflies
Lethargy
Appetite loss

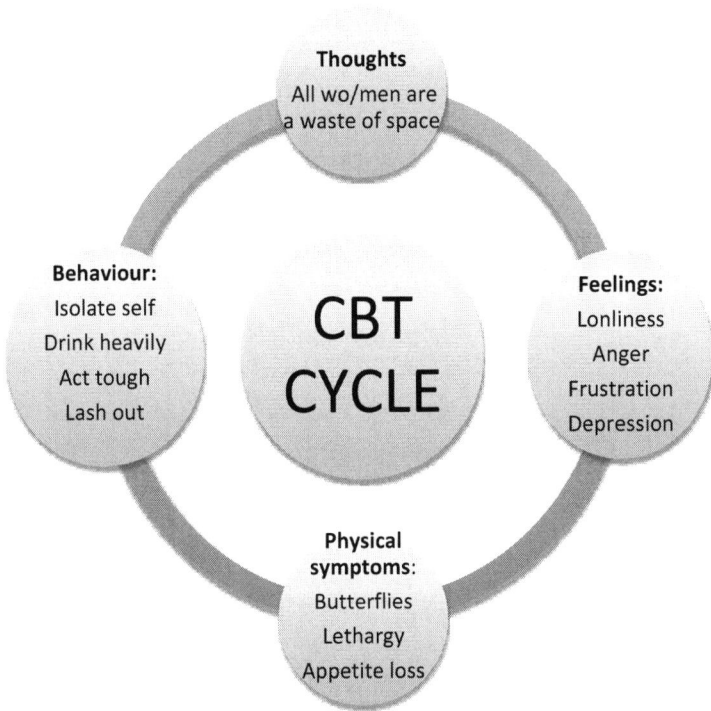

According to CBT theory your thoughts will trigger the negative feelings, and subsequently make you feel physically unwell and then this will impact on your behaviour, which in turn may set you up for further rejection. This will then reinforce the negative thought process.

In other words 'wonky thinking' leads to 'wonky feelings' and these subsequently produce unhealthy behaviours.

What beliefs do you have? List some of your own negative thoughts.

Now ask yourself:

- How helpful are these thoughts to you?

- What masks are they likely to help you to create?

- Now check out if they are true?

- Where's the evidence?

- Ask yourself what would be a more useful thought or belief that is more realistic?

- What evidence or experiences do you have to support this new thought or belief?

"Today I am cancelling mess! Getting rid of confusion that's been hanging around like cobwebs on my ceiling. I am releasing my soul from tiredness and antiquated, meaningless crap! Stepping out of traps that have long been rusted.

I am doing like some companies do when they re-organise, forgiving debts, writing off losses, and establishing good credit for myself. There are simply some things that need to be written off. Some people too! -
Reverend June Gatlin

Now draw yourself a diagram like the following example and see what feelings, physical symptoms and

behaviours that your thoughts trigger.

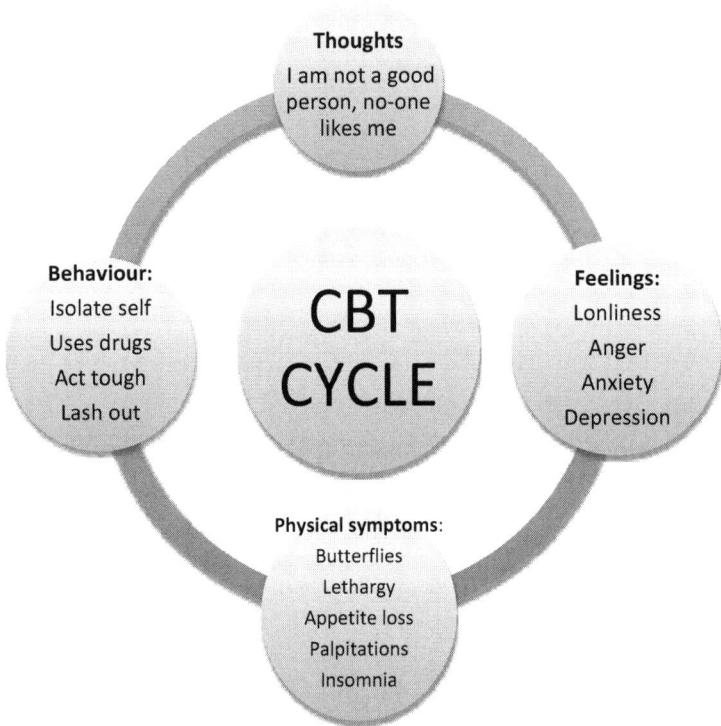

Thoughts
I am not a good
person, no-one
likes me

Behaviour:
Isolate self
Uses drugs
Act tough
Lash out

CBT
CYCLE

Feelings:
Lonliness
Anger
Anxiety
Depression

Physical symptoms:
Butterflies
Lethargy
Appetite loss
Palpitations
Insomnia

Ninety nine percent of the time evidence will show that your negative thoughts or beliefs to be a 'lie!' And yet these thoughts/beliefs, these 'lies' are affecting the way you feel, and how you behave, and helping you to create masks that are a hindrance to you rather than a help!

Often our negative thoughts can set us up for a self-fulfilling prophecy. Suppose you are going to a party and you are thinking "I'm no good at socializing" or "Nobody will like me." Thinking in this way can leave you feeling inadequate and fearing rejection. This will subsequently affect the way that you behave at this party, which may be to avoid talking or mixing, or you may stand defensively. People may see this or sense this and avoid you.

This would then reinforce the thought that nobody likes you. If people do not come over to talk to you, then you will believe it to be because they don't like you rather than it is the way that you are behaving that is putting people off approaching you. However if you reality tested that 'thought' before the party, it is likely that you would behave differently attracting more people towards you.

- How helpful would the above thought be?
- Where's the evidence?
- What might be a better belief, a more realistic one?

A lot of our thoughts are tied up in the past, beliefs that come from our parents or caretakers, which are not necessarily true. Some thoughts we hold on to because of one or two negative experiences, therefore we believe them to be fact. But they are not fact, they are possibly a consequence of our early wounds, or based on a situation that has happened once in the past. They may be based on one persons previous behaviour towards you based on their own transference.

What power we give to all these ghosts of our past!

Let's now look again at the previous cycle using a new belief, a more realistic one:

"I've had a couple of bad experiences with wo/men in the past, however on the whole most people are nice."

Look at the difference this new; more realistic thought would have on feelings, physical symptoms and behaviour:

153

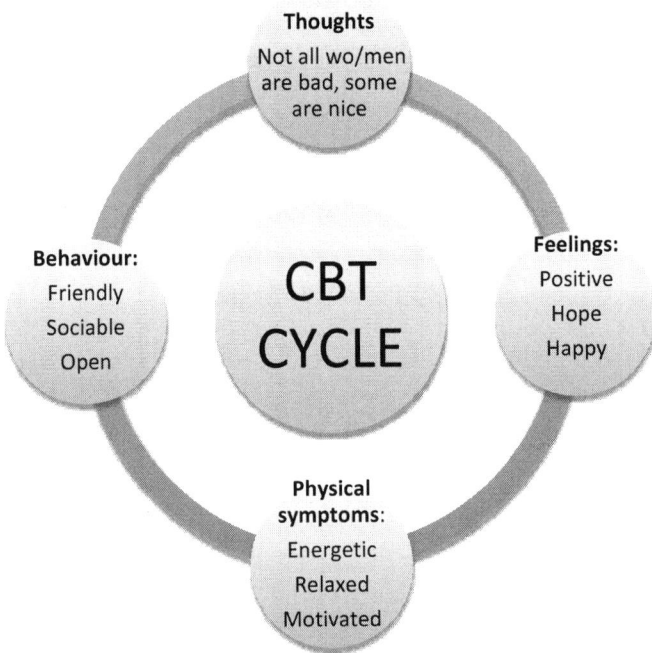

A new belief, a more realistic belief will change your feelings and behaviour.

Think about your own negative thoughts

Practice changing them using this model, and notice how your feelings and behaviour change. Apart from helping you to develop healthier beliefs, it can be fun.

If your thoughts are that you need to be 'perfect' 'strong' 'funny' 'pleasing' to survive this world, then you will set yourself up for failure. Your thoughts will then manifest into "I am a failure,' which will then leave you feeling pretty awful, therefore this will then have an impact on the way that you feel and behave.

So those masks you wear to protect yourself from pain will only create more pain. Let them go.

When you **CHANGE** your THINKING you **CHANGE** your BELIEFS.

When you **CHANGE** your BELIEFS, you **CHANGE** your EXPECTATIONS.

When you **CHANGE** your EXPECTATIONS, you **CHANGE** your ATTITUDE.

When you **CHANGE** your ATTITUDE, you **CHANGE** your BEHAVIOR.

When you **CHANGE** your BEHAVIOR, you **CHANGE** your PERFORMANCE.

When you **CHANGE** your PERFORMANCE, you **CHANGE** your LIFE."

There are many ways of challenging negative thoughts. My favourite is the use of imagery.

Essentially, imagery is any words that create a picture in your head. It is also a term used to refer to any creation or re-creation of any experience in the mind. It is a cognitive process employed by most people.

We have 60,000 thoughts a day, however 95% are the same ones we had yesterday – Deepak Chopra

AND 95% OF THEM ARE NOT THE TRUTH, THEY ARE YOUR INTERNAL BULLY!

Creating your own imagery

To use imagery for challenging your negative thoughts, firstly I need you to think about someone famous, this may be an actress, politician, sports personality or comedian that you really do not like, that you think talks a lot of rubbish and does not tell the truth (bear in mind this will be your perception). If this person entered the room you would walk out, because nothing s/he said would be interesting, honest or make any sense.

Let's use mine and bear in mind, I cannot use real celebrities names in this book for obvious reasons, so I will use a pseudo name

KEITH ORANGE

Now I'd like you to think of someone, who you admire and feel, talks a lot of sense. Think of someone who you could sit and listen to for hours.

SHARON OSWELL

Now choose your own.

The first person (*in my example Keith Orange*) is your negative thoughts, your critical self, you internal bully.

The second person (*in my example Sharon Oswell*) is your positive thoughts, your nurturing self, the self that will challenge bullies, and challenge the things that are not the truth.

Now think about one of your negative thoughts, again I will use one of my own:

Linda you are getting old and wrinkly, there is no point doing anything now at your age.

What is yours?

Now say to yourself "NO this is your bullying person (Keith Orange) speaking, before I believe this to be true I will ask what your nurturing person (Sharon Oswell) thinks. In my example Sharon says:

Linda, everyone gets older but you look pretty good for your age, there is plenty of life in you yet, plenty of opportunities and plenty of skills to put to good use.

- Which thought should I listen to?

- Which thought is the truth?

If I listened to 'Keith Orange' I would feel low, lethargic, and angry, disappointed and may even become depressed. Which would impact on my behaviour and the masks that I wore.

If I listen to Sharon then I will feel good, energised, motivated and calm. It is quite clear which of these statements are the truth and yet most of us choose to listen to the lie, most of us will not challenge the lie.

Before listening and accepting what your first person has said ask yourself what the second person would say then make a choice which one is telling the truth. We don't have to accept what our negative thinking (our internal bully) says, so stop listening to your internal bully!

In this exercise you could use animals instead of people, cartoon characters or any imagery that works for you.

A good idea is to print off several copies of your 'nurturing' person/animal and stick them on the fridge, your wardrobe door, your bathroom mirror, your desk, and in your car as a reminder to 'check out' that negative thought with your nurturing person before believing it.

The important thing is to believe in what your nurturing self says, this is the 'person' most likely to be telling the TRUTH!

If you are thinking more positive about yourself, then your self esteem will be good, you will not need those unhelpful masks and you are more likely to be 'the real you'.

Listen to the bullying devil **OR** listen to the nurturing angel?

It is always a choice.

PERSONAL NOTES & EXERCISES:

Chapter nine

"Letting go of the past"

You cannot erase the past; you must let it go.
You cannot change yesterday; you must accept the lessons learned.
You cannot stop time or stand still in a world racing around in circles;
You must dance with the wind and sing with the songs that are playing.
Let whatever mistakes you have made remain in the shadows of times gone by, and let love be the answer to the mysteries of life.
~~ Author unknown ~~

Most of us have experienced painful times in our lives and often we hang on to this reluctant to let go. We become a victim of this pain.

Hanging on to our thoughts, beliefs, feelings and unhealthy behaviours will set us up for more wounds. And most of all it stops us from getting rid of those damn awful masks that we wear.

You have heard me say on numerous occasions in this book "Take a risk' – what is taking a risk you may ask yourself or how big a risk will I need to take to let go of these masks that I wear? Here are just a few:

- *Learn to laugh more and take the risk of appearing a fool.*
- *Cry and take the risk of being seen as too sentimental.*
- *Get close to someone again and risk intimacy or rejection.*
- *Tell people how you feel and risk them seeing your vulnerabilities.*
- *Share your thoughts and ideas and risk loss.*
- *Love without expecting love in return.*
- *Try something new and risk failure, the person who takes no risks, does nothing.*
- *Open yourself to change.*
- *Stop fearing disapproval from others you only need approval from yourself.*
- *Resolve your anger and stop avoiding conflict. Learn to be assertive.*
- *Face all your problems one by one.*
- *Accept compliments and reject criticisms.*
- *Let go of old beliefs that are not good for you. And start to let go of past mistakes.*

It is time to move on, use our experiences in a healthy way. They help us to understand others, they help us to understand ourselves and they help us to grow into better human beings.

Pain is like a tree being pruned to make it grow strong

If I had a pound for every client I see who has some shame or regret for things they have done in their past which has held them back from doing many positive things in their life now and in the future, I would be a millionaire. They often say that knowing what they have done in the past stops them from moving forward, they use expressions like "I feel like a brand new vase that has been chipped" or "I feel like a broken doll".

They find it hard to believe that people will accept them because of the things that they have done in the past. They say "how can I change, how can I smell of roses when I have been living in garbage"

I say "Why are you letting so much of yesterday use up so much of today?"

We **ALL** have skeletons in our closets. We have **ALL** had thoughts that may be unpleasant. We have **ALL** experienced negative emotions and we have **ALL** behaved in unacceptable ways. We are **ALL** human.

See your painful and shameful experiences in a positive light. Ask yourself:

- What did I learn from this experience?
- How might I prevent this from happening to me again?

- What has this experience taught me about ME?

Let me now tell you the old story about 'a carpenter:'

An elderly carpenter was ready to retire. He told his boss of his plans to leave the house building business and live a more leisurely life with his wife and family. His employer was sorry to see such a good worker go. He asked him if he would build one more house before he went as a personal favor.

The carpenter said 'Yes', but in time it was easy to see that his heart was not in the job. His workmanship was shoddy and he used inferior materials. It was an unfortunate way to end such a dedicated career.

When the carpenter had finished his work, his employer came to inspect the house. He handed the front door key to the carpenter and said "This is your house, my retirement gift to you."The carpenter was shocked! What a shame! If he had only known he was building his own house, he would have done it so differently.

It is the same for all of us. We build our lives, a day at a time, often putting less than our best into the building. Then with a shock we have to live in the 'house' we have built. If we could do it again, we would do it differently. <u>BUT</u> we cannot go back.

You are the carpenter of your life. Life is a 'do it yourself' project. Your attitudes and the choices you make today, build the 'house' you live in tomorrow. Build wisely!

This man could either learn from this experience or spend the next ten years angry and resentful for the mistake he made, which will use up a tremendous amount of energy and stop him from doing more exciting things with his retirement.

The past, your mistakes and your experiences have made you the person that you are today – you have learned a lot from your past that you can take into your future. Use these experiences as bricks and mortar to 'build the house' you now want to live in.

It's never too late to be what you might have been
-George Elliot

It's not only the 'good' experiences that help us to move

forward, the 'bad' experiences can do this more so. People learn more from their failures than they ever do their successes.

However the cause of many psychological ailments i.e. depression, stress, anxiety is people's need to hold on to overwhelming pain, anger, resentments etc, from the past which can then manifest themselves into physical illness. More and more evidence is coming to light now that unresolved psychological problems lead to physical illness.

We carry our feelings around in an imaginary backpack, and each problem or painful event we experience is just added to the bag making it heavier and heavier until it is too burdensome to bear.

Holding on to anger is like holding on to a hot coal with the intent of throwing it at someone else; you are the one that gets burned.

The bag eventually splits and this is when people are unable to function, this is sometimes when people decide to access psychological therapies to help them to work through the items in their backpacks.

Why wait until they split?

These bags need to be emptied on a regular basis.

Spend some time looking at each load you are carrying and list them in order of importance:

> **Example:**
>
> Guilt around dumping an ex boyfriend
> Shame at dropping ice cream on a teachers head and someone else getting the blame
> Not spending enough time with my Gran before she died
> Anger at how I have been treated by an ex
> Guilt about not dealing with my son's problems very well as a teenager
> Not spending enough time with my children when I had the chance

Now we need to start dealing with these issues that are still festering in the background of our lives. We need to empty some of our backpack.

 **Ask yourself:**

✓ Do I want to keep hold of this?

✓ How can I dispose of it in a healthy way?

✓ How is carrying this around with me helping?

✓ What will happen if I let it go?

✓ How can I let it go?

There are lots of ways you can let things go, here are a few:

- ✓ Talking them through in therapy is always useful.

- ✓ Talking through with a close friend and hearing other people's perspective on things.

- ✓ Write someone a letter not necessarily for posting. Sometimes writing a letter helps you to offload your feelings and see things more clearly. This allows you to release the anger. Burn the letter.

- ✓ Write things down and have a ceremonial bonfire of you letter, imagining letting go of the feelings in the flames.

- ✓ Use imagery and send your thoughts or feelings up in a balloon.

- ✓ Use your nurturing imagery learned earlier to challenge the negative thoughts you have about the situation

- ✓ Talk to the person you think that you have hurt in your past, chances are they will not remember or have a very different perspective

- ✓ If you were wrong apologise, either in person or by letter

- ✓ Constructively confront the person you are angry with or whom has hurt you.

✓ Use a Mantra on a regular basis; say to yourself each morning when you get up

"I will let go of the past and move into the future more freely"

These tools work, give it a try and make your backpack lighter.

You build on failure.
You use it as a stepping stone.
Close the door on the past.
You don't try to forget the mistakes, but you don't dwell on it.
You don't let it have any of your energy, or any of your time, or any of your future.
Johnny Cash

We all make mistakes and poor choices but the past is just the past, it cannot be changed, you can only do something about the present. Everyone experiences falling down a deep hole at some times in their life, you can either stay in that hole or climb out, and learn to walk around it in the future.

The past is history. The future a mystery,
The 'now' is a gift because it is the present.

Sometimes we struggle to let go of the past due to an inability to forgive or to forget past hurts or unfairness. People may have been hurtful to us in the past, but do we really want to give them the **power** to destroy our whole lives, to affect our relationships with others now and in the future???

Think about that ex that cheated on you or let you down, do you really want to give him or her the amount of **power** that ten years later s/he still has an impact on your relationships?

Try to look at your mistakes as a 'choice' – for example:

"I chose to have this relationship, with all good intentions, s/he abused my trust, but I have learned such a lot from this. I cannot be responsible for his/her behaviour, nor can I be responsible for the masks this person wears that makes him/her behave in this way. All I can do is move on and trust again, trust myself and trust others. I am not to blame!"

Letting go of hostility, bitterness and resentments towards others will enable you to meet people freely, without transference, and you will then experience more authentic relationships.

To let go of the past and let go of the masks that we wore in the past takes a great deal of courage. <u>You</u> have that courage to declare to the world who you really are!

Love and accept yourself, if you can do this then you can accept that you are human and subsequently accept that to make mistakes <u>is</u> human.

To let go of the past needs you to accept that you are vulnerable, we often avoid being vulnerable due to insecurity, a lack of self confidence or trust in others. It can be very frightening to unmask our true emotions. How many times have you said "I'm never going to let my guard down again!" or something similar. What a shame! No-one is ever going to get to see the 'real you', the beautiful you, the unique you.

We all have a scare about change and what I am asking you to do is change a pattern of a lifetime, change the way you think, feel and behave and change the way you present to others.

The scare we often have is that it might be painful – it is! It hurts in the beginning but then you realize that it is a nice kind of pain, a relief just like you feel after someone has taken a painful tooth out, or a painful splinter, it hurts like hell but then when it is removed you feel a great sense of relief.

Accepting who you are and what you are capable of will help you to let go of the masks that you are hiding behind, the masks that are protecting your vulnerabilities, the masks that are protecting you from past hurts and fears. When you accept yourself unconditionally you will learn how to trust again, you will have the confidence in others to let down your 'strong' mask and show your weaknesses.

Accepting that you are a human being and not some super hero will stop you from trying so hard to get things 'right,' trying to be perfect to impress others, to be accepted, which will only in time set you up for failure and rejection.

This then triggers behaviours such as 'freezing people out,' 'pleasing others,' 'acting tough' etc. This is not who we truly are. We are not then an authentic person, an authentic friend nor an authentic lover.

The time has come to let go of the past. The time has come to say good- bye.

It is not about the disposal of your wonderful memories. It is about the elimination of the memories that are affecting your life, which are encouraging your defenses, which are attributing to your unhealthy behaviours and helping you to develop an unhelpful front.

Part of letting go is accepting and admitting the past is over, done, finished, and complete. Start looking ahead, rather than looking behind.

All that you have been and done was once important, but

now, it is more important to move forward, to grow, and to be all that you are capable of becoming.

Let go of all your pain, false hope, anger, frustration, humiliation, discouragement, and disappointment.

If you do not feel ready, go back and work through some of the exercises in this book, they help you to understand and accept the past and why you have been feeling, thinking and behaving in the way that you have. Once you have that level of understanding and acceptance letting go is the easy bit. Or you may want to book in to see a therapist to support you in this journey.

Don't cling on to it, it's like moving home. Sometimes it is hard to leave as your home is full of memories, good ones and bad ones but still memories that you want to cling on to. But you cannot sell your house <u>and</u> keep it.

It has to go. You can make new memories, nicer ones borne of your new sense of freedom. The freedom to be YOU!

All the strength you need to achieve anything is within you. Don't wait for a light to appear at the end of the tunnel, stride down there........... And light the bloody thing yourself!
- Sara Henderson

PERSONAL NOTES & EXERCISES:

Chapter Ten

"Be who you are"

"Just to be yourself"
The curse of always longing for.
To be somebody else,
When you're not happy who you are,
Or being just yourself.
The days of always wishing for,
That you could be like them,
The ones that cannot ever lose,
The one's who always win.

The moments always dreaming of,
That everything would change,
You wish and hope your life away,
But all things stay the same.
It's such a waste of motion, and
It's such a waste of time,
To live your life through someone else,
It really is a crime.

For you to have such potential, and
You have so much to gain,
By going back to being You,
As you are unique and okay.
The blessing of acceptance, just

To be the one you are,
To live the life given to you
And reach for <u>your</u> own star
Adapted from a poem written by David Ronald Pekrul

To be true to yourself takes courage, it requires you to be introspective, sincere, open minded and fair. It does not mean that you are inconsiderate or disrespectful of others. It means that you will not let others define you or make decisions for you that you are able to make for yourself.

Being yourself means that you like who you are. It means to live life how YOU want to live it, regardless of what other people think. It means that you respect yourself and don't worry about what other people think. You have no control over their thoughts, only your own. Their thoughts come from their own psychopathology and their transference.

In a nutshell being yourself is to be true to your core identity rather than being phony and faking a different one because you think it will be attractive to others. Try to be the best 'you' that you can be.

Remember:

- Love what you do
- Embrace your flaws
- Keep on learning
- Build healthy and lasting relationships
- Don't be too hard on yourself
- Choose to be happy

- Understand that you deserve to be loved
- Start telling yourself what you love about yourself
- Focus less on winning the approval of others
- Distance yourself from those who bring you down
- Forgive your past self
- Start making the changes you know you need to make
- Never stop looking for your own strengths
- Don't be surprised if some of your values seem to conflict
- Avoid focusing on the past and not letting yourself grow
- Relax
- Find yourself and define yourself on your terms
- And last but not least, in the words of Oscar Wilde *"Be yourself, everyone else is already taken"*

As you become more aware of the circumstances in which you wear a certain mask, don't get frustrated with yourself if you can't change your behaviours straight away. You have maybe been wearing these masks for many years, maybe even your whole life. Be patient and gentle with yourself.

The first step in change is simply to watch out for and notice when you are wearing that mask that you want to change. Notice what event or person triggered you to put on that mask. How did it feel when you were wearing it? How did you feel afterwards? What did it achieve? Was there a positive or negative result? What would you like to do differently next time you are in that same situation, so that you are more authentic?

Sometimes with awareness change happens organically. If it doesn't don't pressurise yourself to change overnight. Be compassionate with yourself. Trust in yourself, believe that in time you will be able to take these masks off and that it will feel so good!

💡 **Try drawing your own mask and then a mask of what is underneath that mask**

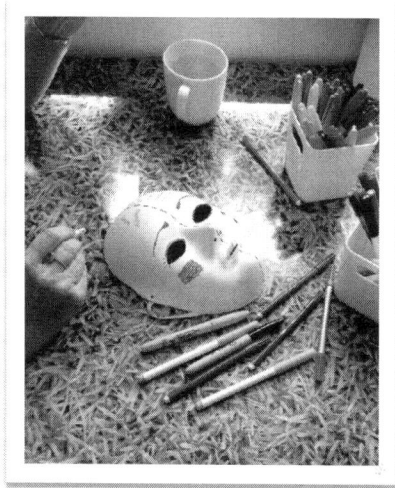

Feelings I can show & feeling I am conditioned not to express

Sometimes for some people, creativity can help you to discover what masks you wear and what is underneath those masks. This is a sample of my attempt on an art therapy group. I found this to be a struggle as I do with all art work. I explored this in the group and remembered an incident when I was around three. I was drawing on a piece of paper on mums leather dining chair. I had a pen and I was stabbing the paper to make dots and unbeknown to me it went through the paper and stained my mum's chair. She was very cross and this was the first stinging smack that I can remember that stung afterwards.

We wondered as a group if the smack and mums anger and disappointment in me, was what stifled my creativity throughout my adult life, the development of my first mask of "Oh I can't draw, I'm just not very creative."

The mask I wear and the hot mess I can sometimes be

As an experiment I stabbed the second mask, like I did as that three year old. It felt really uncomfortable, almost like I was expecting that stinging mask. The rationale was to give myself permission to do this again in a more accepting environment. It was not easy and only time will tell if this opens up my more 'creative self.'

Try it, try creating your own mask with paints, pens, feathers, material, buttons etc.

Here is a consolidation of your learning from this book, each time you feel that your life is stuck, or lots of things appear to be going wrong in your life or at times when you are feeling low, just read through this to remind you of the tools you have learned and the tools you now have, to help you on your journey.

You could use these messages as mantras or posters on your fridge, you can use them as an opening quote when you switch on your mobile phone or on your screensavers.

Often as in therapy, we can get so caught up in life, we can forget the tools we have learned and revert back to our old ways, old patterns, which is why it is important to have some reminders.

Here is a list of reminders.

We are all born free. All our decisions, values, beliefs, defences and masks develop through our experiences of life and the experiences that others put on us. We can at any time change those things if they are not working for us.

We are not going to be understood when we are not open and honest or when we hide behind non-authentic feelings. It is important to be genuine about how we are feeling.

We have learned to adapt our behaviours to suit our own interpretation or misinterpretation of our parental messages.

We have the ability to challenge and change those messages.

We often try to be who we believe other people want us to be instead of being ourselves; it is okay to be YOU!

We attract certain people into our lives because of how we are presenting ourselves to others; this is why we sometimes attract the wrong people for us. We can change the way we present ourselves at any time to attract healthier relationships.

We carry baggage from past relationships into new relationships. A successful relationship is when we meet people freely and leave yesterday behind.

Intimacy is allowing others to see what is 'inside of us'. Practicing intimacy with others encourages them to do the same. We can be intimate and keep ourselves safe from hurt at the same time.

Don't let others try to change you into something you are not, as that only creates internal conflict.

Remember the masks we develop to protect us from pain often cause us more misery.

We write our own life story from an early age making decisions on how we are going to be and how we are going to live our lives, these often develop because of painful experiences. We have the ability to write a healthier story for the future.

We waste an awful lot of psychological energy pretending, wasted psychological energy depletes us from physical energy.

The lower your self esteem the more masks you wear to hide behind, change your thinking about yourself, look at your positive qualities and accept yourself.

Some people will blow your candle out to make theirs shine brighter. Don't let them!

Remember you are unique! Ninety percent of your personal view of self is based on what you think others think of you. You are building your self-concept on the fickleness of other people's opinions!

Having a high self esteem is NOT boasting how great you are. It is quietly knowing that you are worth a lot. Priceless in fact!

You can not change your past, but you can change the way that you see yourself today.

Anyone who has never made a mistake has never tried anything new.

It is impossible to recognise qualities in others unless you have these qualities yourself.

The more accepting you are of self and other's, the less masks you will need to wear.

If you judge people you have no time to love them.

Make not your thoughts your prisons

Treat people as you do your pictures and place them in their best light.

A life lived in fear is a life not fully lived.

The whole of life is a journey and as soon as you know the answers, you get completely lost again.

Turn your wounds into wisdom.

When you live life hiding behind your masks? When you enter phony relationships with phony masks you rob yourself of acceptance, intimacy, freedom, true friendship and true love.

People who reject you for being yourself are not happy with who they are and are not meant to be in your life enjoy your life with genuine like-minded people who accept you for who you really are.

All love that does not have true friendship for its base is like a mansion built upon the sand!

If the video goes wrong, we troubleshoot. If our business is failing, we troubleshoot. How many of us actually troubleshoot our own lives. It's because of this that the same horrible things happen to us time and time again. We don't stop to ask why???

Your thoughts will trigger the negative feelings, and subsequently your behaviour, which in turn may set you up for further rejection. Reinforcing the negative thought process. In other words 'wonky thinking' leads to 'wonky feelings' and these produce unhealthy behaviours.

Ninety nine percent of the time evidence will show that your negative thoughts or beliefs to be a 'lie!' And yet these thoughts/beliefs, these 'lies' are affecting the way you feel, and how you behave, and helping you to create masks that are a hindrance to you rather than a help!

A new belief, a more realistic belief will change your feelings and behaviour.

We have 60,000 thoughts a day, however 95% are the same ones we had yesterday – Deepak Chopra

The important thing is to believe in what your nurturing self says, this is the 'person' most likely to be telling the TRUTH!

If you are thinking more positive about yourself, then your self esteem will be good, you will not need those unhelpful masks and you are more likely to be 'the real you.'

Why are you letting so much of yesterday use up so much of today?

We <u>ALL</u> have skeletons in our closets. We have <u>ALL</u> had thoughts that may be unpleasant. We have <u>ALL</u> experienced negative emotions and we have <u>ALL</u> behaved in unacceptable ways. We are <u>ALL</u> human.

We build our lives, a day at a time, often putting less than our best into the building. Then with a shock we have to live in the 'house' we have built. If we could do it again, we would do it differently. <u>BUT</u> we can not go back.

You are the carpenter of your life. Life is a 'do it yourself' project. Your attitudes and the choices you make today, build the 'house' you live in tomorrow. Build wisely!

The past, your mistakes and your experiences have made you the person that you are today – you have learned a lot from your past that you can take into your future. Use these experiences as bricks and mortar to 'build the house' you now want to live in.

It's never too late to be what you might have been

It's not only the 'good' experiences that help us to move forward, the 'bad' experiences can do this more so. People learn more from their failures than they ever do their successes.

Holding on to anger is like holding on to a hot coal with the intent of throwing it at someone else; you are the one that gets burned.

The past is history. The future a mystery, the 'now' is a gift because it is the present.

Try to look at your mistakes as a 'choice'

To let go of the past and let go of the masks that we wore in the past takes a great deal of courage. You have that courage to declare to the world who you really are!
Love and accept yourself, if you can do this then you can accept that you are human and subsequently accept that to make mistakes is human.

Accepting that you are a human being and not some super hero will stop you from trying so hard to get things 'right,' trying to be perfect to impress others, to be accepted, which will only set you up for failure and rejection.

When you accept yourself unconditionally you will learn how to trust again, you will have the confidence in others to let down your 'strong' mask and show your weaknesses.

Let go of all your pain, false hope, anger, frustration, humiliation, discouragement, and disappointment.

All the strength you need to achieve anything is within you. Don't wait for a light to appear at the end of the tunnel, stride down there........... And light the bloody thing yourself!

PERSONAL NOTES & EXERCISES:

AUTHORS NOTE

Well I have come to the end of my book. I hope that you have enjoyed reading it as I have enjoyed writing it.

I took a risk, a big risk to do something that I wanted to do. When I did my counseling diploma twelve years ago, I said *"If I do not pass, it does not matter, I have learned more on this course about myself and about others that will benefit me for life, that is what is important to me"*

I feel the same about this book. *"If it never gets published, it does not matter, I have left behind an heirloom for my children and grandchildren, messages and education to help them to hopefully have fulfilling lives and encourage them to be themselves in a world that is continually trying to 'change us'.*

And who knows it may fall into the hands of someone who needs it, someone who is very unhappy at the moment, someone who is in pain or someone who is trying hard to change but needs some help. If this is you, then I hope you have the tools now to be yourself, you are unique and beautiful.

I'm now going to wear purple with green fluffy slippers, a hat full of fruit and blow those massive bubbles in the middle of Asda. I hope to see you there too!!

Always be true to yourself

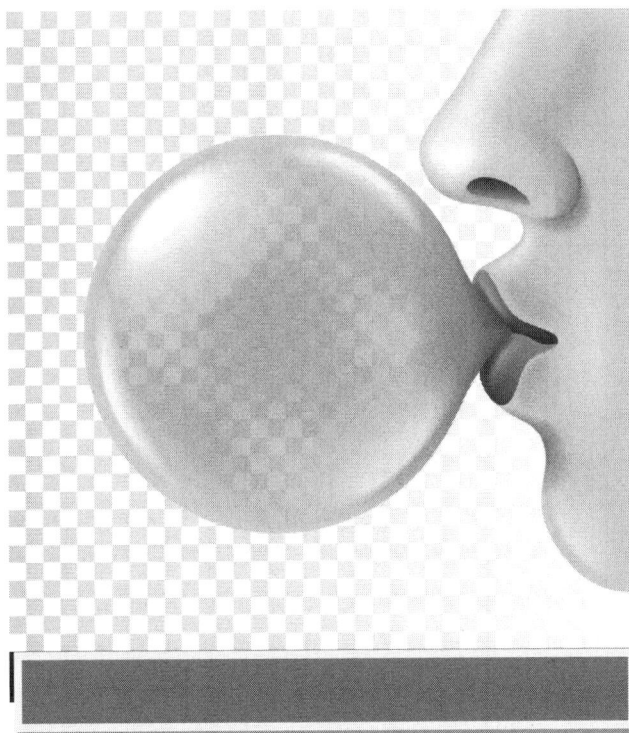

I shall wear purple

Further books since published by this author:

Self help books

I shall be blue

I shall be clean

Teenagers are from Pluto

Children's book

The fairy on top of the Christmas tree

Crystal Magic

The mystery behind Grandpas chair

Friends in the rain forest

Novels

Gut Instinct

A woman's world

Jane, me and myself

The Haymaker

Text Books

An Introduction to counselling skills and theory

Training Manual for Certificate to Diploma in therapeutic counselling

Counselling and psychotherapy training – Level 4

COMING SOON!

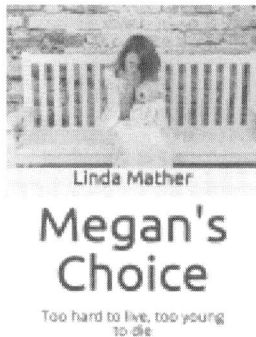

Linda Mather

Megan's Choice

Too hard to live, too young to die

Available on Amazon August 2019

Printed in Great Britain
by Amazon